HOW TO BE YOUR DOG'S SUPERHERO

Published by
www.elitepublishingacademy.com

First Edition published 2016
© Dominic Hodgson

Printed and bound in Great Britain by
www.n2printondemand.co.uk

A catalogue record for this book
is available from The British Library
ISBN
978-1-910090-62-6

PRAISE FOR HOW TO BE YOUR DOG'S SUPERHERO

What dog trainers are saying about How To Be Your Dog's Superhero

"Dominic's book should be of great help to anyone who is having problems controlling their dog – the biggest reason that dogs end up in animal charities in the UK."
John Rogerson, Dog Trainer and Behaviourist
www.johnrogerson.com

"What a well-written, entertaining, and thought-provoking read. This book will challenge much of what you know about dogs, or think you know. It will encourage you to look at things more from the dog's perspective than from your own and just might give you a whole new, more wholesome understanding of your 'best friend'."
Robert Alleyne, Dog Trainer and Behaviourist
www.thedogownersclub.co.uk

"At last, a book which doesn't require a dictionary or a degree to understand. No jargon, just dog training at its finest that dog owners can understand. Thank you Dom for showing people how simple dog training can be and explaining that bonding and friendship with your dog are the most important things. A most enjoyable read."
Marie L Holt, RVN, MBVNA, NCert (AnBeh), Dog Trainer
www.inlinedogtraining.co.uk

"I wasn't long into the preface when I realised this book was going to be a lot more fun to read and relevant than many of the dog training books available! Follow the advice given in this book, and your dog will very soon become your best friend and companion, and after all, that's why we have dogs, isn't it?"
Alison Burgess, KCAI, Dog Trainer
www.wheelgates.co.uk

"The world of dog behaviour and training is held in some kind of mystique by many. It doesn't need to be unless there are serious issues such as aggression and fear, which are often linked! However, even with fear and aggression, often if the owner simply understood that coexistence with the family dog can be achieved easily and without the need for dogs chasing everything they see, often including other dogs, then even some of the more serious behaviour concerns would never arise.
Dom, well done. This is a very clearly written book and will help to guide those that read it as to how to have a great life with their family companion dog or dogs."
David M G Davies, Canine Behaviour and Training Advisor
www.daviddaviesdogtraining.com

"If you are serious about improving your dog's behaviour and recall for the better and, more importantly, improving your relationship with your dog, then this is the book to read and follow. Very sound advice."

Bev Smith, Dog Trainer"It makes such a refreshing change to read a book that puts the emphasis on play, and having fun with your dog, to improve the bond between you both to help facilitate training.

How To Be Your Dog's Superhero is a wonderful and entertaining read, and the information is given in an easy-to-follow format that you can work through step by step, knowing that your dog will be having fun as you go."

Emma Setterfield, Dog Walker"This is an excellent training manual presented in a very humorous and accessible manner. Dom certainly understands many of the problems that a companion dog owner is likely to come across when trying to live in harmony with their dog. He also describes the causes and the solutions to these problems. These solutions, if followed, should indeed lead to a fantastic relationship between dog and owner. Or as Dom puts it, by using the training methods in the book you will become your dog's superhero. That is something all dog enthusiasts would love to see, as it would mean more under-control and happy dogs with equally happy owners!"
Fiona Henderson, Dog Trainer
www.solihulldogtrainingclub.com

"This is a very well-written book with snippets of humour, which keeps you wanting to read more. It is an ideal book for those who own dogs, be it experienced or new owners, but equally a good read for those who are thinking of becoming dog owners.
If dogs could recommend a fun, enjoyable, and informative book, this would be it!"
Jemima Hitchen, Lecturer in Animal Care Studies, East Durham College

"Dom's book is entertaining, funny, and actually helps with what I'd call 'real world' scenarios in today's dog training. As dog trainers we are so often consumed with science and using the correct terminology that we forget to transfer it in such a

way as to help the wider audience. This book is straightforward with witty real-life stories and advice on how to get a better relationship with your dog. The games and activities mentioned throughout the book will help put the right building blocks in place so your dog starts to look at you in a completely different light – and a shining light at that! The book title aptly describes just what you should strive to be for your dog, and you owe it to your dog to take the time to read this book!"
Rebecca Ashworth, Dog Agility Trainer
www.northumberlanddogtraining.com

"Finally a book that is easy to read, informative, with some humour mixed in too. This book is a fun and educational read that anyone with a puppy or dog should get. It's clear and easy to understand. If you follow the guidelines in this book, you will have a better canine companion because of it. It's worth every penny and more, and I highly recommend it."
Joe Kelly, CTDI, APDT, IACP, Dog Trainer

"From the outset it was obvious that this book was going to be different and refreshing.
I read a lot of dog training books, many of them written in the same old styles either full of scientific jargon or in the 'fluffy-bunny perfect world' way that just makes me put the book down there and then.
This book, thank goodness, is neither of these. It is simple, easy to follow and most importantly realistic and downright entertaining.
Good work Dom! I look forward to the follow-up."
Rachel Bean, Qualified Veterinary Nurse and Canine Behaviourist, RVN BVNA MCFBA MTGODT

What dog owners are saying about Dom and How To Be Your Dog's Superhero

"This book is different to other training-your-dog books, as it helps you first of all to understand where 'you' are going wrong to cause your dog's unwanted behaviour. I've had some realisations that have already changed my relationship with my younger dog for the better, and I'm looking forward to putting the plan of action fully into practice."
Lin Armstrong (Poppy and Barney)

"This is a very well-written, straight-to-the-point, essential survival kit for anyone, anywhere who owns a dog. There are some real quick wins as well as long-term training plans and lifestyle choices to make sure your very much-loved pet and best friend shares your life in the nicest possible way. And it is enjoyable for both of you."
Lucy Garside (Aster and Dexter)

"*How To Be Your Dog's Superhero* is a clearly structured, often humorous dog training book that is full of common sense. It is a book to dip into or read from cover to cover, which is something I know I will do many times!
From the 'Preface' to 'The hunger games', each chapter covers clearly how best to approach the problem faced. It gives fantastic hints and tips and caused me to have many 'Why didn't I think of that?' moments. It is enthusiastically written and shows clearly Dom's experience and excitement for the subject of making life for our dogs the best it could possibly be. My favourite chapter has to be 'Finding the Kryptonite', which teaches you how to play with your dog. It's so easy when you know how and is something that has probably made the most difference to us.
This is a book I wish I had been able to read when our

Cocker Spaniel, Ruby, first came to us. We have had many problems over the years, often exacerbated by well-meaning but often bad advice.

Learning how to be Ruby's superhero has made a terrific difference to me. It has removed the feeling of failure and guilt of being an inadequate dog owner. It's given me freedom to have fun and know my dog is happy. We play and happily do our own thing.

We have followed the 'My Dastardly Dog' online dog training programme for eight months and have made huge strides forward. This book provides a great overview of this programme. I now have the hard copy by my bedside to dip into whenever I want. It is a perfect fit for me.

It is a book that has long needed to be written. It brings Dom's humorous and common-sense approach to dog training to many more people. Buy this book!"

Edwina Freeman and Ruby

"I first came across Dom online six months ago when I was looking for some ideas to make myself more appealing to our young working Cocker, Rocket. Although he was super affectionate and lovely natured at home, when we went out for walks it was becoming increasingly obvious that I was irrelevant to him, and I felt that I really needed to do something to change his focus from following his nose to looking at me. He was not interested in playing with me at all at the time, especially when we were out and about. But after working with Dom's advice and making a real fool of myself on a regular basis, we managed to start fooling around together, first at home, then in the garden, and then in the field.

It's been a long haul and we're not where I want to be just yet, but we've made so much progress. He now looks at me to see what we are going to do next. We can play with a ball or

Frisbee and lots of 'find it' games, and having that playing base has allowed us to start getting so much more out of agility, gun dog and scentwork training. And best of all it has been really good fun! You can tell when your dog is really enjoying being with you and having a good time, and then so much more seems possible."
Ellen Cooke and Rocket

"This book will give you a true understanding of why your dog acts in a certain way, and Dom gives you the answers to put this right. It is simple but very powerful. I can truly say if you continually follow Dom's instructions, you will have a) a happier dog, b) you will enjoy your dog more, and c) have lots of fun! My Cocker is a testament to Dom's methods and hard work, and this book shares the secrets of how it is done."
Lindsay Ledger and Lily

CONTENTS

PREFACE

Congratulations… and welcome to my world. By buying this book you've taken the first step towards having a more enjoyable and stress-free life with your pet dog. It's time for you to leave behind the frustration and guilt you feel when you have to tell your dog off for pulling on the lead or running away from you in the park.

Taking your dog for a walk should be the highlight of your day, and I want to help you make it so.

It's no exaggeration to say that what follows over the next 200 pages will have a profound effect on the way you live with your dog. I will help you understand why your dog does the bloody annoying things he does.

Better yet, if you are in the small percentage of people who do 80% of what I recommend in this book, then very soon your dog will gaze at you like a 10-year-old boy meeting Spider-Man. Not only that, he will follow you around the park like the Pied Piper and ignore the empty pizza boxes, birds, dogs, or any other distractions you may come across.

The truth is anyone can be their dog's superhero

I got my first dog when I was in my twenties, and since then, I have made every mistake that it is possible to make with my own dogs. My dogs used to pull on the lead like a train, and many times I have stood waiting in the rain with nothing but a dog's lead for company while they were off enjoying themselves, oblivious to my frantic calls for them to come back. You are definitely not the only one that has happened to.

I promise you I love my dogs as much as you. Heck, I also make my living from working and training them.

I know, therefore, how frustrating and embarrassing it can be when they do all the bloody annoying things they do.

I should point out now that throughout the book I will be referring to your, my, and everyone else's dog as a he or him. I'm aware there are female dogs, but I will be sticking to the male reference for no other reason than I own two male dogs and, well, it's my book. I found it easier to refer to dogs as simply he or him rather than he/she and him/her, or 'god forbid'… it. If that's too controversial for you, then you should probably put the book back now because you will hate the rest of it.

I have a little secret for you

Dog training is much easier than you think, and **you** really can be your dog's superhero. You can be the person he loves, listens to, and wants to be with the most, not only when he is being cuddled on the couch, but everywhere you take him.

You may have guessed by now, but this is not your typical off-the-shelf theory and history of dogs. If not, it's best I don't waste your time, by telling you right now that it isn't. The last thing the world needs is another long, boring, jargon-filled theory of dogs written by a dog trainer for other dog trainers to pore over.

Not this book

How To Be Your Dog's Superhero exists for one reason and one reason only. That is to help pet dog owners connect, bond, and have fun with their dogs. Dog ownership should be fun. No one ever got a dog because they wanted more stress in their lives, yet that's what owning a dog is like for many of us.

And you shouldn't feel guilty about wanting your dog to be better behaved either. It's natural to feel jealous of the other well-behaved dogs that you see at the park. I felt like that too. And I know from working with my training clients over the years that most dog owners suffer from the same problem. They own a dog they love passionately, but they have little control over the dog because he doesn't listen to them. I also know how to solve this problem in a fun, easy, simple-to-understand way, which is also challenging for the dog.

I promise I will transform the relationship you have with your dog. I will take away the guilt, frustration, and helplessness you feel when it comes to controlling and training your dog. I like things to be simple for me and my dogs to understand, and I'm sure you do too.

When I say promise, it does rather depend on a couple of things...

Firstly, if your dog can't read, and I know that he cannot, then you will have to implement everything in the book. You are the only one who can change your dog's behaviour. I know this will disappoint some people who expect things to happen by magic, but all I can do is share my experiences and guide you through the lessons that within time will take you closer to being a superhero dog owner.

It's up to you to do the work!

I don't really do 'sugar coating' either, so if you are a sensitive snowflake who believes that the world runs on pixie dust, then you definitely won't like this book. Despite what you have seen on the TV, you can't just magic or dog-whisper away your dog's bad behaviour. It takes understanding, a plan, and then action.

Secondly and most importantly, we need to put the FUN back into owning a dog. We all enjoy ourselves and learn better when we have fun, and our dogs are no different. Dogs live to play and have fun, but sadly most dog owners don't play a big enough part in how their dog enjoys himself. The dog then has to find his own outlet for having fun, which often isn't something we want it to be. Once I discovered the secrets of how to play and really have fun with my dog, then the way I trained, influenced, and enjoyed him changed almost overnight. That is the opportunity you have now too.

So where do we begin? How can you have fun with your dog and stop him jumping up, barking at the postman, or running away from you in the park? Well, for starters you need to BMFI.

Be More Fucking Interesting

Yep, if you want to be really loved by your dog, then we need to make you more appealing to him than the passing pigeon, the bulldog, the cheese pasty on the ground, or the pee-covered lamp post.

This doesn't mean donning a pair of red underpants and a cape next time you take him to the park. I will show you simpler and more socially acceptable ways to BMFI, so you can be your dog's superhero.

Don't worry if you think your dog doesn't like you or that he won't do anything for you at the moment. I will show you how to find out exactly what makes your dog's tail wag. Then we will use that information to play with him and influence and train him to do what you want. Prepare to have your eyes opened too. I once taught a pug to swim using a feather, but I will share more on that story later.

Remember, anyone can be their dog's superhero and that includes you.

So with the preamble out of the way, if you're up for the challenge, then let's leash up and begin.

INTRODUCTION

It's estimated there are around a half-billion dogs in the world (including strays) and nine million pet dogs in the UK. The World Canine Organisation (Fédération Cynologique Internationale) estimates there are 339 actual breeds of dog in the world today.

But did you know there are only two kinds of dog owners?

The first group has dogs that truly love them almost *all of the time*. They enjoy the company of their owners and tend to stay near them wherever they go. The next group has dogs who would often rather be anywhere else than with them and the further from the sofa they go, the less interested they seem to be in their human keeper.

Perhaps unsurprisingly, the owners in group one have dogs who hardly ever have any recall or reactivity problems. They take their dogs for stress-free daily walks anywhere they choose, they can enjoy a coffee or an ice cream at a cafe with their dogs, and when they can, they take their dogs on holiday with them.

The second group endures a different kind of dog-owning experience. When they go for a walk, their dog can usually be found in another part of the park altogether, where they may be eating poo, chasing pigeons, or more likely looking for and playing with their doggy friends. That's if their owners can find them at all. You see, while these dogs very much enjoy you whispering sweet nothings in their ear while you cuddle them on the couch, they quickly forget their name and often turn stone deaf as soon as you step outside your house. For the poor owners in group two, every trip to the park, beach, or woods has the potential to be a very stressful affair. They feel as if they are constantly telling the dog off for ignoring them, and it's a daily battle of wills.

The owners in group two don't love their dogs any less than the owners in the first group; they actually love them very much. But for some reason the dogs don't feel the same way. There is a lack of connection; but how did this happen?

Getting a dog was supposed to be the thing that would complete your family and give you a reason to enjoy long relaxing walks in the park. This was the family member that would never grow up and leave home. So how did 'man's best friend' become 'that bloody dog' for so many of us?

Before we tackle that, I do have to ask: which category of owner do you fall into? Does your dog follow you around like you are the Pied Piper, or like many owners, do you have trouble getting his attention when he is sniffing a pee-covered lamp post, never mind when another dog appears?

What I'm really asking is: would you say your dog loves you and listens to you all the time? Or only when it suits him, and there is nothing else around that he finds more interesting?

If you are currently in group two, then don't worry, because I used to be too, and I know it wasn't much fun at all. In fact, it was a bloody nightmare. Yes, I, too, have stood alone in the park holding a dogless lead while I shouted for my dog to come back. He did eventually, but only when he had finished saying hello to every other dog he met.

I am going to show you how you can get your dog to listen to you and do what you want him to, even if at the moment, your dog would far rather chase something that has grabbed his attention. This superhuman power that you need to get your dog to look, listen, and pay attention to you can be described with another word.

The dirtiest word in dog training

I'm referring to the dreaded 'c' word. No... not that one. I'm talking about 'control'. Having great control of your dog is something all dog owners should have, but it doesn't mean dominating your dog. It doesn't require you to shout at him or use an e-collar or a check chain. You don't need any of those things, but if you want to be a responsible dog owner, you bloody well do need to have very good control of your dog. Especially if you are exercising your dog off leash, and yes, all dogs need off-leash exercise.

So control is key. For one thing, the Dangerous Dogs Act (UK) demands you have great control over your dogs in public and private places. And there are hefty fines and possible prison sentences if your dog is deemed dangerously out of control.

The law is obviously important; however, the responsibility that dog owners have to their community and to future dog owners is equally important. As hard as it might seem to believe, not everyone in the world likes dogs, and people who don't like dogs certainly don't want dogs running up and bothering them. More out-of-control dogs will mean more dog-control orders and less public spaces to exercise and enjoy our dogs. And a world without dogs would be a very sad place indeed.

So now that we have got the 'c' word out of the way, and I'm warming to my task, why don't I shatter a few more myths about dogs – myths that seem to have wormed their way into the way we think about dogs? If you are very sensitive, then this will ruffle a few feathers, and by ruffle I mean pluck out and shred.

Harsh unpleasant truth number one

It's not the dog's fault

This is a big one and it's worth repeating, so I will.

It's not the dog's fault.

Your dog doesn't go out of his way to do things to annoy you. Dogs are clever, but they aren't that clever.

- ◎ If your dog runs away, it's not his fault. He should have been on the lead, or you should have been more in control.
- ◎ Your puppy poops on the floor. Not his fault I'm afraid, you should have let him outside quicker.
- ◎ Your dog jumps up at someone and knocks them over. Not his fault either. And neither was it the person's

fault. Jumping up is something he has learned to do, and it's your job as his owner to teach him not to do annoying things like that.

◎ Your dog pulls on the lead so hard he makes your palm sore and regularly embarrasses you. Yup, you guessed it; that's not the dog's fault either.

◎ He may have ripped the wallpaper off the walls when you were at work and pinched your dinner while you were pouring a glass of wine, but remember…

It's not the dog's fault!

Hey, we are all human though, and you can still feel pissed off when he does any of those highly annoying things (I know I do), but it's a waste of time thinking that your dog did them on purpose. Also, getting angry or upset with your dog will just confuse him and won't lead you any closer to a situation where he does something better instead.

You need a plan to help you teach your dog to do something else. We will look at exactly why dogs do things that drive us crazy in the next chapter, but for now just repeat after me 'It's not my dog's fault'. Treat it as a mantra every time the shit hits the fan and the next time your dog commits a crime that has you palm-slapping your face.

Accepting this one truism will have a profound effect on the way you think and feel about your dog's behaviour. By accepting responsibility for his actions, you put yourself in the liberating position of being able to do something about it.

Harsh unpleasant truth number two

Your dog only needs one friend

And that friend is…

YOU!

Which means your dog doesn't need to have any 'doggy friends'. In fact, the more dog friends he wants to play with, the harder he will be to exercise and control.

I appreciate not everyone wants to hear this information and the more 'touchy-feely' you are, the harder it will be for you to take, but this is real life and not a Disney movie. If Lady and the Tramp had been real-life dogs and had sat down to that romantic meal, Lady would have told the Tramp to piss off in no uncertain terms and would have eaten all the spaghetti herself.

The truth is your dog can and should get all the friendship, love, stimulation, and exercise he needs from you, his owner.

What this book isn't

How To Be Your Dog's Superhero isn't an obedience book, showing you how to teach your dog to sit and stay (although we do cover that). This is a guide to help you to enjoy your dog all of the time. Yes, it requires you to train your dog, but the emphasis is always on YOU and YOUR dog having fun. So if the thought of training your dog is about as appealing as washing your hair in a bowl of dog vomit, then don't worry, this is going to be FUN. I have hopefully set this book up for you to succeed, and all your dog and I need is your enthusiasm.

However, this book is not for you if you are someone who likes reading but never puts anything into action. Anything you learn you will have to implement. The great news is I know the very person to help you train your dog. It's someone who has time to spend playing with and training your dog, they know quite a bit about him already, and they actually love him more than anyone else in the world.

Yes, it's you, dear reader. Believe it or not, you are absolutely the most suitable candidate to take on the role of your dog's superhero.

I have made this very easy for you to do by giving you bite-sized chunks of information, which are wrapped up in stories with real-life examples, and there are lots of challenges and exercises for you to complete throughout the book.

Don't think for a minute you can't make the leap from average owner to your dog's superhero. I don't have a degree in dog psychology, I'm certainly not a bloomin' dog whisperer, and I didn't even own a dog until I reached my twenties. And I haven't always trained dogs the super-easy, kind, and effective way I do now. In fact, when I look back now, I'm quite ashamed of the way I've pulled and shouted at my own dogs in the past when I was less well educated. I share this to let you know that I am human and I have made many mistakes just like you. It's a horrible feeling to shout at your dog and know that he doesn't like it, but not know what else to do.

The good thing is it's never too late to turn over a new leaf. Rather than feel guilty about shouting at your dog, let's do something positive to change things, because a better life together for you and your dog is closer than you think.

Look, I know you love your dog. I don't know exactly how much, but I'm guessing a lot, because I'm a human being who loves my own dogs too. But is love enough?

Well, if your idea of loving your dog involves just looking at him and cuddling him on the settee in the evening and not taking much responsibility for how he lives the rest of his life, then this book won't suit you. In fact, instead of a living, breathing animal you should probably have bought a teddy bear or a nice picture of a dog to keep you company, instead.

However, if by loving a dog you mean sharing your life and playing a full and active role in providing all of the things your dog truly needs to be happy, then you are in luck because all these things can be quite easily achieved using the methods I describe.

How to use this book

Once you have read this book from cover to cover, you will have a great idea of where you may have gone wrong in the past. You will know exactly how to avoid the situations that cause your dog to be naughty, and you will have a solid plan to follow to allow you to move on.

The ultimate prize

If you do the things I suggest, the ultimate prize that awaits you is a great one and that is... freedom.

No, I'm not getting all *Braveheart* on you here; it really is freedom.

I know you want the same things as I do and that is for your dog to love you and for him to want to be with you. You want to be able to take him anywhere and be relaxed, knowing that he will stay near you (and out of trouble!). Well, if you have a dog that does this, then you have the freedom to enjoy your dog wherever you go.

Do you have freedom? Does your dog want to be with YOU all the time, everywhere you go, no matter who else is around? Or does he just show you love when he is at home, getting cuddles on the couch or when it's time for food?

Imagine being free to enjoy off-lead walks with your dog in the park, free from the stress of not knowing if your dog is going to come back to you if you let him off his lead. Imagine being free to walk your dog in public without the embarrassment of him barking or lunging on the lead every time he sees another dog.

This is the freedom that my clients and I enjoy now with our dogs, and that freedom awaits you too.

Confidence is key

When I was struggling with my dogs' behaviour, I felt like a bit of a failure as a dog owner. My confidence and belief in my own ability to train was quite low, and yours may be too. I want to help you grow in confidence over the coming days, weeks, and months, so you believe in yourself and feel confident that you can not only bond with, play with, and train your dog but also control him in a way that you and your dog will enjoy.

I have set up the exercises within the book so you can have a go in an environment in which you feel comfortable, such as your living room. This way you can get some quick wins under your belt, which will give you some momentum. Any new experience we enjoy and repeat often becomes a habit, and I want you quickly to get into the good habit of enjoying playing with your dog.

Let's have a look at exactly how we got where we are right now.

CHAPTER 1
HOW DID YOU GET HERE?

Many dog owners seem to suffer from the same kinds of problems, and perhaps unsurprisingly, one of the reasons is they all make the same kind of mistakes with their dogs. These are mistakes that I and every other dog trainer have made once upon a time too. Mistakes are natural and nothing to be ashamed about. We get better by making mistakes, and they are part of the learning process. But to learn and get better at something only happens when we recognise where we have gone wrong. Then we can try something different.

In this chapter, we are going to look at some of the main mistakes that you (and me and everyone else) have made with your dog. Even if you made them with the best intentions, they are still mistakes and repeating them is going to hold you back, so as uncomfortable as this might be, let's find out how you got where you are now. To put you at ease, why don't I put my hand up first and admit to some of the prize clangers I have made with my dogs.

My big fat dog training mistake

In 2011, I left my job of 10 years as a sales rep for a FTSE 100 company. It was an enjoyable enough job and it paid the bills, but I didn't really want to do it for another 20-plus years. Call it a midlife crisis if you want, but I'd had enough and wanted to do something else. I also knew I definitely didn't just want to dive into a similar job in sales, so what was I to do?

Well, I'd had enough of working indoors, so a job with access to fresh air was a must. My main interest at that time was dogs. I had this germ of an idea to start my own business where I could combine the two, and people always say you should find a business doing something you love, don't they? But still, I was a little afraid of telling Beth and the kids that I wanted to start a dog-walking business in the middle of a recession.

In my spare time I had been walking some of the dogs that were awaiting adoption at my local rescue, and it was around then that we adopted our Dogue de Bordeaux, Barry. Now don't start giggling, because the name suits him! Getting an 18-month-old rescue dog came with some challenges, and I had been reading a lot of books about dog training to give me the tools to help Barry settle in.

When Barry came into our lives, he was a big ginger ball of energy. This is often the case with rescue dogs, and one of the main reasons dogs are given up is because they don't get enough exercise, and they can then become unruly and destructive. The Dogue de Bordeaux is not a breed that is known to be high energy, or so we were told. So to get rid of the pent-up energy Barry had, I did lots of exercise with him. We walked a lot. We jogged together too. We cycled, again with him jogging alongside rather than on a tandem! I bought him a doggy backpack too, which he really enjoyed wearing, and he used to pull much less when he wore it.

So with some rather patchy success with exercising and training Barry under my belt, and my love of being outside in sun, sleet, hail, and snow, I convinced myself, and then Beth and the kids, that I would start my own dog-walking business. Well, a dog-walking business with a difference. I wanted to offer more for dog owners than just a walk around the block. I didn't know much, but I knew that dogs that had some good exercise every day would generally be better behaved and sleep better. I hoped there would be people like me who put a value on a service that offered high-energy adventures for dogs. So that's what I did.

In Sunderland we are blessed to be a 10-minute drive away from beautiful beaches, parks, woods, and plenty of countryside. So I used to pick up my clients' dogs, and we would have an adventure somewhere different every day. We soon got into a routine of hiking for an hour or so, and then I would let the dogs off lead to have a sniff and a toilet break. But this little break wasn't so chilled out for me.

When the dogs were off lead and had finished their sniffing, some of them would start to play together. They seemed to enjoy this and, I will be honest, I didn't mind too much either, as it gave me a chance to get my breath back. However, the playing quite quickly became a problem, and I was finding it really difficult to get the dogs back on lead again. The downtime had become party time for them. They were having such fun playing together, and they needed me less and less. I was finding it more difficult to get them to listen to me at all, even when I shouted at them. This escalated to the point where I didn't want to let them off lead at all, because I knew when I did, I had little control over them.

So, on the advice of a friend, I attended a seven-day intensive dog behaviour course with John Rogerson, who, if you didn't know, is considered by many to be the forefather of modern dog training. On this course I also met another dog trainer, David Davies, who would become my doggy guru and great friend too. The course changed everything for me and set me on a new path that I never knew existed. It was here I learned that I should play with my dogs if I wanted them to listen to me and want to be with me.

From that week on, I made sure that I was the one who provided the fun for my dogs and my clients' dogs when we were adventuring. I led the games we played. Now, instead of messing about together, the dogs looked to me, the human, for play and entertainment. And because I had their attention, I had much more control. And more control meant they could enjoy even more off-leash exercise and freedom because I could get their focus quickly back on me whenever I wanted.

My story is not too dissimilar to what many pet dog owners have been through, and it may mirror your story too. The consequences of allowing your dog to become too interested in anything else but you are exactly the same as they were for me. If you have spent a lot of time socialising your dog with other dogs, then that is something he will enjoy. Not only that, but he will remember that he enjoyed it, and he will seek out other dogs every time he gets the opportunity.

Unfortunately, dogs tend to generalise and they can soon see every other dog they meet as a potential playmate. This results in dogs pulling and lunging on the lead to get to other dogs, or even just to get to the smell of another dog on a pee-covered lamp post. Often this frustration at not being allowed to get to the thing they want can build and lead to aggression.

Of course, this problem isn't always exclusively other dogs. Your dog may be interested in birds, cats, joggers, or kangaroos (if you live in Australia). If it's exciting enough for him, then your dog can learn very quickly to enjoy chasing or playing with anything. It doesn't even have to be a living thing. With little else to stimulate him on his daily walk, your dog could enjoy chasing leaves or cars or he may just enjoy finding piles of fox poo to roll about in. Don't underestimate how silly or disgusting dogs can be if they find it enjoyable enough.

And it may not even be a thing at all. I have met many dog owners whose dog's favourite game is running away and not letting his owner put the lead back on. No one would ever knowingly teach a dog something like that; I hope not anyway. This is much like a child who experiences the manic laughter that comes when you blow a raspberry on his tummy and then cries, 'Again, again again!' So it only takes a couple of times for your dog to dodge your outstretched hand and to experience the same frisson of excitement and think, 'This is fun, again, again, again!'

The dog who runs away like this isn't thinking to himself 'Oh I know what I will do today. I will run away from my owner; that will really piss him off!' No. The dog does this because

HE enjoys it. It's fun. The fact that it annoys you is just a by-product of the fun. Dogs quickly learn through trial and error that it is a bloody fun game and it's even worth getting told off for, when he is finally apprehended.

The result is you have a dog that is much more interested in doing something else than he is in being with you, his owner.

Many of the problems that dog owners experience come about because they have allowed their dogs to become too interested in things that don't involve them. And most dog owners are not aware of the number-one truth of dog behaviour, and that is…

Dogs are selfish!

Now by selfish I don't mean that your dog wants to become leader of the pack, take over your house, and make you sleep in the yard. No, by selfish I simply mean dogs learn to enjoy certain things, and then, given the opportunity, they will choose to do those things as often as they can.

Most dogs love running, digging, sniffing, eating, and playing. And depending on the breed, your dog may also like retrieving, herding, swimming, cuddling, pointing, or tracking as well as many other activities. The point is that dogs all have different desires, and if taking part in their favourite activities doesn't involve you, then unfortunately you have just made yourself an irrelevance to your dog. I did just that with my original adventure dogs.

This mistake is made by many if not most dog owners. Most of us when we own a dog bump into other dog owners at the park. If the dogs are off lead, they might end up having a little play together, which they very much enjoy. If this is repeated often, then the dog soon learns the park is the place he goes to have fun with other dogs. You the owner then become nothing more than a chauffeur, much like the parent who takes their kids to the funhouse to play with their friends. But dogs aren't kids, and we need to stop pretending that they are.

I remember when my eldest son, Alex, who was 14 at the time, decided he didn't want to go to the match on a Saturday anymore. Well, he still wanted to go, but with his friends instead of me. I was gutted, but what could I do? Children have to grow up and do new things that don't involve us as much. As it happens, my youngest, Toby, started coming with me the next season, so I had no let-up from supporting Sunderland at all!

But there is no need for your dog to be like that. Dogs are more predictable and much easier to look after than kids. It's less likely your dog will want to follow his best doggy friend if **you** are his best friend. And as long as **you** provide everything your dog needs to be happy and tick all the little boxes that appeal to his selfish nature, then looking after him and keeping control will be a doddle.

So where are you with your own dog? I have a few questions for you that may help you decide where you are right now...

How much does your dog pull on the lead?

1) He doesn't pull at all. He walks perfectly and even tells me when to stop, look, and listen.
2) He pulls me very little. He may get distracted by a passing pizza box, but I can easily call him back to heel.
3) He's a puller alright. He is better on the way back from the park, but on the way there he is very excited and pulls a lot, and it hurts sometimes too.
4) Walks with my dog are a test of strength, and one I frequently lose. He has always pulled me to the park and back again, and on the way I have to avoid other dogs because he is very reactive.
5) After a walk with my dog I feel like a gorilla, and my arms hang limply by my side. Walking my dog is no fun at all. I hate the fact I can't enjoy taking him out.

What is the first thing he looks for when you let him off lead in the park?

1) Me, me, and only me. My dog is locked onto me like a heat-seeking missile and he never leaves my side; in fact, I can't get rid of him!
2) Me, mainly me. He likes to wander off for a sniff, but I don't mind as I can easily call him back to me. He loves playing with a ball with me.
3) He looks at me a lot but is quite easily distracted too. If he sees one of his close doggy friends, then he will choose him over me.
4) My dog loves playing with other dogs, and when they are not there, he loves looking for them. He is difficult to exercise off lead because of this.

5) My dog forgets me and his name as soon as we get to the park. Exercising him is a real struggle, and I don't enjoy it very much at all.

How did you do then? Were there more fours and fives answers than ones and twos? Don't worry about the ones; they are for perfect dogs. I don't have a perfect dog, and as you will find out in the next chapter, there isn't really any such thing. But if you scored a three or more, then there are lots of things we can do to help you to BMFI to your dog!

How?

First things first...

The first thing you absolutely must do is to stop your dog from doing the thing you don't want him to do, and we do that by tackling the problem head on, and avoid it completely. Yes, the easiest way to stop your dog from chasing dogs, rolling in fox poo, or pulling on the lead is to not let him do it in the first place. So you don't exercise him off lead, or let him off so he can roll around, and you don't walk him on lead if he pulls.

The second thing is to teach him to do something more pleasurable instead. And this is the point where most dog owners and some dog trainers get it wrong. They try and force a new regime onto a dog without taking into account any of the dog's likes or needs. This does work, but you will achieve much quicker and long-lasting results if you are able to influence your dog using things he already likes. Why? Well, because he already likes them, of course.

I'm not one for going shopping any time of the year, and I especially hate wasting time in long queues. I prefer messing about with a dog in the countryside, as you well know. But I'm much more agreeable to going Christmas shopping with my wife if she promises me a trip to the pictures to see a movie I like, or a slap-up meal at my favourite restaurant when we are done. The key there is a movie I like or a meal at **my** favourite restaurant. Yes, I'm selfish too. We all are, and so are our dogs.

Knowing the fact that your dog is selfish will change everything for you. It will enable you to move forward rapidly with your training, and here's how.

Mini case study

Two of my earliest clients were Lindsay and Duncan and their Cocker Spaniel, Lily. Lily had learned through trial and error that running away from her mum and dad was the best thing ever. In fact, she enjoyed it so much that they didn't dare let her off lead. Even Duncan had enough after he allowed Lily some off-leash play inside a fenced-off running track area, and it took him two hours to get Lily back. It was at this point that I was called in to help out. So using the two-step method, I first stopped Lily from being able to run away from me. I used a two-metre lead that I let trail on the floor so I could easily get control again. This plan had to be modified to using a five-metre lead when Lily realised that as long as she stayed about two metres away from me, she could evade my capture too.

Next, I knew that Lily liked tennis balls, so my task was to convince her that it was more fun to bring them back to me than it was to run off with them. This took a while, because the unwanted behaviour had been practised by Lily for a long time. It was just a game to her and she enjoyed it. But by using praise and affection, I was able to convince Lily that giving me the ball back was more fun than running off with it.

So I turned the tables on Lily and tapped into her selfish nature by using something she loved (the ball) to get her to do something I wanted (not run away). I did this without using a check chain or an e-collar or any punitive methods at all. The use of the long line was key, though, as it prevented Lily from running away while I taught her something new. Finding a way to stop your dog from behaving badly is essential, and at first avoiding it altogether is the easiest way to go.

So we are going to do things a little differently to how you may have trained your dog before, because your dog is unique. He has different likes and wants than any other dog, and so what works for someone else's dog may not work for yours. And you are going to find out exactly what your dog likes. Knowing and using this information will change the game and make influencing and controlling your dog much easier.

Stacking the deck

Imagine playing poker and knowing exactly what cards every other player has and when they are going to play them. That would not only make winning much easier; it would make losing virtually impossible. Every time you had a bad hand, you could just fold and go again in the next round. That's what you will be able to do with your dog by the end of this book. You will quickly identify the triggers that make your dog do the bad things he does, and then you will avoid them. Knowing how and what to teach your dog is paramount, but knowing what situations to avoid so you make it as easy as possible for your dog to learn something new is also vital.

The success sequence

If you have ever studied any martial arts, you will know that when you join a new club such as a karate club, you always start with a white belt. It doesn't matter if you did some taekwondo when you were a kid or even if you were the heavyweight boxing champ of the world; everyone starts with a white belt. In many ways, the white belt is the most important belt of all. It represents the beginning, and the moves you learn and perfect from here form the basis for all future belts.

I myself was a white-belt dog owner and trainer not so very long ago, and I know how confusing and frustrating it can be when you don't know how to get this dog you love to do what you want him to do. For what it's worth, I'm still on my journey too, and I'm certainly not a black belt yet.

So, you must not skip ahead searching for the silver bullet that will solve your problem. You couldn't just walk into a dojo and say 'Oh, I like the look of that purple belt. I think I will give some of that a go.' And so it is with this book.

First, I will get you connecting with and understanding your dog through the games we play. And we play lots of games! We play because it's fun, and we all learn better when we have fun. You will learn what your dog likes to be rewarded with, and he will learn what he has to do for you to get those rewards. Once we get that in place, we can really start motoring, and you can begin to teach your dog some alternative behaviour traits that will help you solve the issues you are currently having.

But in the beginning, it's a white belt for everyone, so just accept it, wear it with pride, and enjoy the journey.

So what is the easiest way to train a dog? Good, I thought you would never ask!

In my opinion, the absolute easiest, safest, and most fun way to get your dog to do anything is to make him WANT to do stuff for you. By make him, I don't mean using mind control or even forcing him to do it, but rather influence his selfish nature by using things he is already interested in. Yes, finding out what your dog is already interested in is the easiest way to connect with, train, and live happily with your pet dog.

I know that sounds way too easy, but the best ideas are always the simplest, and here is a little story to prove it.

In 2007, the World Health Organization (WHO) implemented a change to operating procedures, which led to deaths on the operating table falling by 40% and the rate of major complications in surgery falling from 11% to 7%. This might sound like a very small percentage change, but experts estimate the number of lives saved across the world could be as much as half a million!

So what was the change?

Was it more training or better equipment? More advanced medicine or more doctors and nurses? The answer may surprise you.

It was a checklist.

Yes, a bloody checklist.

Some bright spark simply looked at the number of errors that were contributing to deaths and decided that it would be a good idea to trial a simple one-page checklist that takes just a few minutes to complete.

All of the members of the surgical team, surgeons, anaesthesia providers, and nurses, started to perform key safety checks before, during, and after the surgery. These included checking that they were operating on the right patient; in fact, they deemed that one so important it was on the checklist twice! And in my unqualified medical opinion, it is always a good start to make sure you are operating on the right patient.

But this proves that the simplest and most obvious changes can deliver truly amazing results.

And it did this by helping the professionals to eliminate mistakes. By mistakes I don't mean getting things wrong, because that's just part of life – we all make mistakes, even me – but if we can create a situation where you make fewer mistakes with your dog, then he will learn much more quickly what it is you want him to do. And it will be less frustrating for you too.

The biggest mistake most pet dog owners make is they expect too much from their dogs too soon. They attend a training class, and after a couple of lessons they have their dogs walking really nicely to heel and even managing to weave in between chairs in the village hall. Then they take their dogs to the park, and the whole thing goes tits up because the dogs are far too interested in all the sights and smells to want to play the silly heel game with their owners.

I'm not having a go at dog training classes here, but anyone can teach a dog to sit. I could wear a blindfold and hold a piece of chicken in front of me and listen for when my dog's bum hits the floor and throw the chicken to him. Boom, I just taught a dog to sit. So teaching a dog to sit (or wait, or heel) in a boring church hall is one thing. Teaching a dog to be able to focus on you and do a 'sit' when you are at the beach and there are a dozen dogs running around and the ocean is beckoning him to have a splash is something else. To be able to enjoy your dog truly, you need to be able to do both and everything in between.

So you need a system that allows you to build up gradually, and that's what you will be doing in this book. First, I will teach you how to get your dog's attention at home and then in your garden, before you move on to your back lane and eventually the park. And at each stage, you are going to be having fun and playing with your dog and showing him what a superhuman dog owner you really are.

This way of learning will take all the pressure off you. It gives you a chance to be free of any inhibitions you may have about playing with your dog, which you may have in a training class filled with other dogs and people. And it also gives your dog the best opportunity to learn somewhere with minimal distractions. And it makes teaching your dog FUN again. If you avoid the situations where your dog misbehaves and is distracted, then he won't ignore you and you won't get annoyed.

I know what you are thinking: how do I avoid my local park or taking my dog for a walk?

Well, you stay inside. Yes, your dog needs exercise, but I am going to teach you how to exercise him at home and in your garden. Staying in with your dog, for a week or two, and removing the distractions from the equation will give you an opportunity to bond with your dog somewhere you feel safe. Your home is the best place to begin connecting with and training your dog. Not outside where there are a gazillion smells for him to sniff; even a group dog training class environment can be too distracting for many dogs.

Think about it for a minute. If you can't easily get eye contact with your dog and play with him, train him, and have some fun with him in your own living room, then what chance do you have of doing so when you are in the park and a pheasant flies out of a bush or a Golden Retriever comes bounding up to you both? So for now, think no walks, no worries. I hereby absolve you of any need you may feel to make your life any more difficult than it needs to be.

Some will heed this advice and others will not, but the people who do what I recommend and begin the training at home will, I promise, have the most success. I'm not saying you aren't going to walk your dog or take him to the park ever again, but you need to progress to that over time. Remember it's white belt first, and for you that means learning how to get your dog's attention and make his tail wag.

In the next two chapters we will look at what we want from our dogs and also what they need from us to be happy. It's a shorter list than you might think.

Chapter summary

- The biggest mistake most pet dog owners make is allowing their dogs to enjoy doing stuff that doesn't involve them.

- Dogs are very selfish creatures. Just like us humans, they like doing things that make them happy. The more we involve ourselves with how our dogs get their daily kicks in life, the more relevant we become to them.

◎ Avoiding and removing distractions from your dog's life and beginning the training at home will make the learning so much easier and more fun. If offered the choice of learning to ride a bike on glass-covered concrete or grass, which would you choose? Hmm, tricky one that, cut hands or a bruised bum. Grass it is! It's the same with training your dog.

You will make mistakes with your training; I encourage you to. It's the only way to grow, but a mistake in the park will probably end up with your dog exhibiting his usual naughty behaviour and you feeling like a bad owner. Start small.

Training task:

They say the eyes are the windows into the soul, and eye contact for us means attention. If your dog is looking at you, then he is listening to you, so I want you to start rewarding eye contact with your dog. Every time he looks into your eyes, tell him he is a good boy and give him some praise and affection. Start right now; say his name and when he looks at you, tell him what a good boy he is and how much you love him.

As an experiment, I tried this with Beth, and her reaction was 'What have you done...?' But I'm sure you won't experience such cynicism with your dog. Dogs love attention, so start now and reward him with a smile and some praise every time he looks at you.

This is the first of several training tasks that I will be giving you, and I'm starting with a nice easy one to get you started. The more times you reward your dog for giving you eye contact, the more he will want to do it. Imagine how cool it will be when your dog's default position is to look at you like you are his superhero.

Think of it like putting money in the bank. Little and often is the best way to save money, and the best way to connect and build an amazing bond with your dog is to reward him little and often, so it becomes a routine you both enjoy. So start saving today!

Training test:

For a further challenge, see how long you can maintain your dog's eye contact by just talking to him. Is it easy or hard? How much harder is it when you are outside with him or just in the kitchen holding his food bowl? For the next day or so, test how readily your dog gives and maintains eye contact with you, at home, in the garden, yard, and on a walk. Make a note of where you struggle, and we will revisit this soon.

CHAPTER 2
WHAT YOU NEED YOUR DOG TO DO

"If you eliminate smoking and gambling, you will be amazed to find that almost all an Englishman's pleasures can be, and mostly are, shared by his dog."
– George Bernard Shaw

Suppose I asked you to design a dog. What would a perfect dog look like to you? Do you picture your own dog or maybe a dog you grew up with? One man's Doberman is another man's Shih-tzu, and we will never agree on what a perfect dog should look like. So, look beyond the physical appearance, and let's think about what we would want a perfect pet dog to *act* like. If you were sitting at the drawing board with Mother Nature, what desirable traits would you want from a pet dog?

See, most of us when we purchase or adopt a dog have a very clear idea of what kind of dog we want. And with squishy-faced Bulldogs and athletic Vizslas, Great big Danes or tea-cup Chihuahuas, there are plenty to choose from. But how much thought do we give to what we want the dog to act like?

I think there are some common desirable traits that we should all want from any dog, no matter what breed they happen to be or what our personal circumstances are.

Life in the 21st century is pretty fast paced for most of us, and our pet dogs now have to compete with many more other distractions we have in our lives compared to 20 or 30 years ago. And although we humans are busier than we have ever been, dog ownership has actually increased in the last 40 years. Owning a dog should be something everyone can enjoy, but finding time in our schedule to give our dogs what they need to be good pets is getting harder.

So… what exactly do we **need** our pet dogs to do?

Not much, you might reply, and you would be quite correct, but not much is very different to nothing at all. We will cover what a dog needs in the next chapter, but knowing what we need our dogs to do will help us to mould them into the kind of dog we need them to be. And there's a very good reason why you should want to do that.

Many thousands of dogs are placed into rescue centres every year, and sadly many of them don't ever leave. Dogs first became man's best friend around 30,000 years ago, so they aren't a particularly new invention. Why then are we so irresponsible that we feel we can treat our four-legged friends just as we do our throwaway clothes, phones, and cars?

And before you say that you are different and would never give up your dog, don't worry; I believe you. But I reckon all of the people who have made the decision to give up their dogs didn't think for one minute that one day they would be doing that when they first got that dog or puppy. I'm not saying it's right, and I personally think anyone who gives up a dog is pretty selfish. There will be very few cases where putting the dog in a rescue centre really is the only option. It's more likely they are getting rid of the problems that the dog is causing them, and if a little more thought had been given to how the dog was going to fit in with their life, then a lot of problems could have been avoided.

This chapter is designed to get you thinking about your dog and what you like and don't like about him. Before you have a fit, remember you can still love your dog AND want to change some things about his behaviour. This does not make you a bad owner; in fact, it makes you a very sensible one. So does your dog chew your shoes when you leave him at home? Is he a nightmare to take on a walk? Are you fraught with worry every time you even think about letting him off lead? These types of problems affect a lot of owners. They will hopefully not be annoying enough for you to consider getting rid of your dog, but they are still bloody annoying nevertheless. How much more pleasant would your life be if you could fix them, or even just manage the situation better?

I've come up with four desirable traits (or DTs) that I think every pet dog owner should want their dog to have.

These are my guidelines, which you can add to if you wish. But remember I am looking at this from the point of view of a dog trainer, who sees a lot of the common problems people have; a dog walker who feels a responsibility to the people in the community that their dog is reasonably well behaved; and a dog owner who likes an easy life with their dog.

Owning a dog should be fun and challenging, but not so stressful that you wish you hadn't bothered. So in an ideal world, what DTs would a great pet dog have? Here is my first.

Your dog needs to be happy to be left alone

I know what you are thinking. Dom, you are one cold-hearted bastard; we haven't even started training the dog, and already you are talking about leaving him on his own! Well, hear me out first.

Most of us have jobs that require us to be out of the house for eight hours every day. That's apart from doing school runs, shopping, and any other activities where we can't take our dogs with us. And unless you can afford a dog nanny 24 hours a day (and if your dog is well behaved, I will happily apply for the job), then your dog is unfortunately going to be home alone for a certain period of time.

And if your dog **is** going to be left alone, it would be nice if he was happy enough with that arrangement not to feel the need to remove wallpaper from the walls or shave the table legs while he waits for you to return. Separation anxiety is very common, and destructive incidents like this are bad enough, but they do only affect you, and you can always just redecorate and buy a new table.

A much worse outcome is if your dog is barking or howling and disturbing your neighbours. This can cause a lot of bad feeling, and if it escalates can even lead to prosecution. But anyway, as we already said, it's just not cool to have your dog bothering other people in your community, which includes your neighbours.

Let's not forget the dog in all this either. No one wants to think of their dog being stressed and upset at home. I miss my wife a lot when I'm away from home for any length of time, but I would be at my wits' end if I knew she was pacing the floor or destroying the sofa while I was away. To my knowledge this has never happened!

We all want our dogs to be happy, and if your dog is displaying signs of stress when you leave him alone, then you are naturally going to feel guilty about it. Your dog has the unique ability to make you feel guilty as hell for leaving him alone and, at the same time, also incredibly pissed off with him because he has chewed up your Jimmy Choos.

Separation anxiety is a problem that a lot of dog owners experience. And it can be a contributing factor when owners give up their dogs for rescue because they feel the dogs have become too difficult to manage. We can learn two things from this.

The first is how little thought the average new dog owner gives to how a dog is going to fit into their lives. I'm just guessing here that most people don't acquire a dog on a Monday and then on Tuesday they get a new job that requires them to leave the dog alone most of the day. You need to give a new dog or puppy time, but you also quickly need to get them into a routine that works for you and them.

The second point highlights how easy it is for new dog owners to get things very wrong, even when they have the best intentions.

Teaching a dog not to have separation anxiety

It's common for new dog owners to take a week or two off work to bond with their new dog. In that time, they will fuss and coo at the dog almost non-stop, especially if it's a puppy. Who can blame them; puppies are damn cute. But perhaps it's no surprise that your dog is more than a little confused when you suddenly go back to work and his routine changes dramatically almost overnight.

Now, left alone for long periods of time with nothing to entertain him, it's no wonder that the dog will start to chew furniture or whine and pine for his owner. Over time this whining can progress to howling, and as the dog gets bigger and his jaws stronger, he moves on from slippers and books to door frames and table legs. In just a few months, the dog has become impossible to live with, and many will be given up at this point.

So if you can teach a dog to be dependent on you to the point of stressing out, then surely you can teach him to be happy to be left alone. Absolutely you can, and not only that, but you should too. You should make it a priority for your dog to be content when you are not there. This isn't optional, even if you don't work and are able to spend every waking hour with your dog. What happens if your circumstances change or you want to go on holiday? Will you find someone who is willing to spend every waking hour with your dog like you do? That's highly unlikely, and they certainly won't be keen to look after your dog again if he ever damages their own house when they popped to the post office. Much like with kids, you tend to be more forgiving of your own than anyone else's.

It's much easier to teach a puppy to be happy being left alone than an older dog. But then it's often easier to teach things to a puppy than an older dog. An older dog has lots of behaviour traits that he has picked up over the course of his life so far, whereas a puppy less life experience and so fewer bad habits and more of a clean slate.

But you can teach an old dog new tricks, and here are some very easy ways you can start teaching a dog to be happy left alone. First you should make sure he has had enough exercise to allow him to want to settle easily. If your dog is a bundle of energy first thing in the morning, and many dogs are, then you need to provide an outlet for the energy he has. Don't expect a dog to just sleep when you leave for work in the morning if you haven't helped him to wear himself out. Playing a game that increases his heart rate and makes him concentrate should do the trick. Then leaving him with something to do should also help. I'm thinking more treat dispenser than iPad here, but I will go more into the magical world of doggy food dispensers in a later chapter.

So having a pet dog that is happy to be left alone is not only something you should want, but something you can achieve too. You will notice a recurring theme in what DTs I think a great pet dog should have, and that is they all should make your life easier. I like to keep things easy and you should too – easy means not difficult, and who wants a difficult dog?

Easy to exercise

I'm sure you are the same as me in that when you first got your dog you looked forward to enjoying long walks in the countryside together. This dog was going to give you a reason to regularly get out there and enjoy the great outdoors. This was my reason, and it was the reason I started my own dog adventure business too.

Enjoying a long walk with your dog is truly one of life's great pleasures. Walking is not only physically good for you; it takes you away from the worries of your job and gives you a chance to recharge and de-stress. For me it's more than just an opportunity to unwind and get some much-needed exercise. I find walking regularly with your phone turned off really puts you in touch with nature. As long as you dress appropriately, it doesn't matter if it's sunny or stormy; you just roll along with the ever-changing seasons. Snowdrops pushing through in spring and the falling of the leaves in autumn become part of your own personal calendar. Of course, this only happens if you are walking a dog that is *easy to exercise*...

If on the other hand you have a dog that prefers running away from you every time you let him off lead because he has seen a rabbit or a squirrel or one of his doggy friends, then you probably won't notice any of the nice things about nature at all. Walks for you will be quite stressful and full of worry, and it might not take too long for you to begin to dread your daily walks with your dog.

How do you exercise a dog easily?

Hopefully you gave some thought to the exercise needs of your breed of dog before you got him, but regardless of the breed, it's much easier if you have a dog that likes retrieving, or playing tug of war or another game that involves you. A Pointer will usually need more exercise than a Dachshund, but you can get high-energy dogs of any breed, and it's much easier to tire a dog if you can control how much he runs around and gets rid of his energy.

If you can control what your dog likes playing with, then you can play that game with him at home or in your garden as well as the park, beach, or woods. This is particularly useful if you work and you need to exercise your dog more efficiently on a morning when you have less time.

At the weekend you can enjoy a two-hour stroll through the woods, but during the week when you are much busier, your dog will still be happy with a shorter walk and some games in the house or garden. Basically as long as his daily exercise quota is being met, then your dog won't mind how he gets it.

Being able to control and influence a dog using treats, toys, or the games you play means you can enjoy more freedom with him too. If he is more interested in you than birds, rabbits, or other dogs, then you will be able to allow him more off-leash exercise. This is what I was striving for when I started my dog adventure business. The feeling you get when you know you are the most interesting thing in your dog's life is truly amazing, and it's something I want every person who reads this book to be able to experience. We can ALL be our own dog's superhero.

Easy to control on and off lead

Unless you live in your own private gated community, then you are going to have to exercise your dog in public places where you will encounter potential distraction and hazards.

In urban areas this will mean other members of the public and other dog walkers, and in more rural areas you will probably experience more sheep, deer, and other wildlife, although the lines between the different areas of our country are becoming ever more overlapped.

So if we know that no matter where we live we are going to encounter distractions when we venture out of the front door, why do we seem to have so many reactive dogs that want to pull on the lead every time they see a sheep, squirrel, dog, bird, or man on a bicycle? Because we allow them to do it.

Dogs are natural chasers, and if we want them not to pull, run, lunge, or react to things that move, then we need to teach them something else to do instead.

Why do dogs pull on the lead? They pull on the lead because it works. It gets them to the park where their friends and the pee-covered trees and bushes are.

Why do dogs run off at the park to chase birds and other dogs? Again, they do it because we let them. We give them nothing else to live for, and we allow that to be the most exciting part of their day. And they enjoy doing it so much that it's worth them doing it even if they get shouted at by you, when you eventually get them back on lead.

We all have slightly different motivations, and our dogs are exactly the same. Why do some people queue up overnight to ensure they get concert tickets or turn up at a department store at 5am on the 26th December so they can get the pick of items in the Boxing Day sale? They do it because they want to, and the prize for them is so great that it's worth doing. Someone else who isn't as bothered will quite happily either do without or just pay the full price later. Being your dog's superhero means you have to be his friend and teacher. Then, he will want to be with you at the park and will not be distracted by other dogs, squirrels, etc. Once you achieve that, then you have a dog that is easy to control on and off leash and is safe around other people and animals.

We hear people using their dog's friendliness as a badge of honour or an excuse for unruly behaviour, all the time. As their dog bounds towards you, knocks over your child, and proceeds to get your dog whipped up into a frenzy, they use the old 'Sorry, he's just really friendly!' Well, no he isn't, I'm afraid. I'm a dog lover and even I think he's a bloody menace. So to have a dog that is well behaved in public, it is better if your dog isn't too interested in people, dogs, or any other animals.

Most of our dogs lead pretty boring lives and often the things that excite them are the things that we don't want them to do and which will get them into the most trouble.

This comes about partly through a lack of knowledge, which you will remedy by reading this book, and partly because we humanise our dogs. Your dog simply doesn't need a wide circle of friends like we humans do. He can get all of his fun and fulfilment from you and the other members of his human family.

A dog that is easy to control and OK around other dogs and people is a pleasure to own, and you will actually spend more time enjoying the outdoors if you have a dog like this.

So that's the list of DTs **we** would like from our dogs, but what about the dog himself? What does he want from life? If we are going to share our home with these creatures, then wouldn't it be helpful to know what makes them happy?

Well, the list of things that a dog needs to be happy is almost as short as the DTs one. And that's exactly what we are going to look at in the next chapter.

Chapter summary

◎ Decide what you want from your dog. The clearer you are about what you want, the more determined you will be to follow through with any training you do. Of course, you may be unsure whether you even want a dog at all now. Let's face it; if you don't like being outside or think it's not your responsibility to play with, train, and look after your dog, then you probably shouldn't own one. But assuming you are OK with those responsibilities, this is your opportunity to stick your flag in the ground and say, 'yes, this is what I want my dog to be like'.

◎ Most of us work, and unless you work from home, it's likely your dog is going to have to be left alone for a period of time each day. It would be desirable then for you to have a dog that is happy to be left home alone. By happy, I don't mean he will be organising house parties and inviting his pals round as soon as your car leaves the driveway, but we at least want him to be content to be alone while you are out. You should take steps to teach your dog that being alone for appropriate amounts of time is nothing to worry about and just part of life.

◎ Think about how much your life has changed in the last 10 years: you may have got married, moved house, had kids, or changed jobs. What's in store for the next 10–14 years, which is the average life span for a dog? Your circumstances may change at any time, so you have a responsibility to your dog to make him as easy to live with as possible. You will have no trouble finding someone to look after your dog if he is easy to look after and exercise; in fact, you will probably have friends and relatives fighting over who gets to look after your dog.

Exercises:

If you have some different DTs to mine, then make yourself a new list, but remember the more things you add, the less successful you will probably be in achieving them all.

Here I would like you to list three things that your dog does that you wish he didn't. Changing things is going to take a bit of time, but the sooner you identify what you want to change, the quicker you will be able to use the methods in this book to help you get there.

So if you could wave a magic wand like Harry Potter, what annoying behaviour traits that your dog has would you like to make disappear?

1)

2)

3)

WHAT DOES YOUR DOG NEED?

"Dogs are obsessed with being happy"
James Thurber

Our Dogue de Bordeaux, Barry, was adopted by us when he was 18 months old, and he arrived with an unusual habit. He used to do something we dubbed 'The crazy run'. The crazy run would generally involve Barry periodically running around like a lunatic as he tried to send his body in four different directions at once. The most predictable moment for him to perform said crazy run was right after he had a done a poo. At first we found this quite amusing, but it soon stopped being funny. After a few weeks, I realised that not only did I not know which direction he was going to run, but it seemed that Barry didn't either. So poo time became something of a hazard, and anyone in the vicinity had to be prepared to play dodge the Barry.

His excitement grew and he would become more out of control each week, so eventually I did the sensible thing and started to put him on a lead when I noticed him crouching into the toileting position. Problem solved, I thought, until the day my dad took Barry for a walk, and I forgot to tell about the new on-lead poo routine. As my dad went to pick up Barry's deposit, unbeknown to him, Barry had set off on a big crazy lap of the park and had built up enough speed to send my dad flying into the air when he crashed into the back of him.

I tell this story in part because it makes me chuckle, but also to prove the point that if a dog like Barry can get this much pleasure out of doing something as mundane as his daily poop, then dogs in general must be pretty fun-loving creatures.

And while it might not be all they want, FUN is pretty high on most dogs' daily to-do list. Dogs are unique in the animal kingdom in that they never really lose their love of playing. Yes, they mature and get older, but if a dog likes playing, then he will continue to enjoy it until he is too old to take part. What or who your dog plays with, though, will have a big impact on his behaviour, and it goes without saying that a dog who loves playing with his superhero owner (that's you by the way) will be much easier to control and live with.

In the last chapter we had our say on what we wanted our dogs to do, but now it's his turn to fill out the wish list. So hand your dog a pen and ask him to write down all of the things he needs to make him a happy hound. I'm kidding of course; a pencil will do just fine... No? OK, why don't *we* make a list for him, and first we will cover a nice easy need that every dog should have fulfilled.

A suitable diet

It should go without saying, but all dogs need nourishing food and fresh water daily. Generally, two meals a day is considered to be better than just one big meal, and certainly two smaller meals will be easier on your dog's digestive system. There are many ways you can and should use your dog's food to make his day more interesting and your life much easier, and we will go into this in more detail later.

What your dog eats can influence his behaviour, and sometimes a change in diet can have an immediate effect on how a dog behaves, but these cases are the exception rather than the rule. Diet and a dog's health are topics you can write an entire book about, and this isn't that book.

You should do some research about what alternative dog foods there are available, but remember that most people who try to sell you anything are doing so with their own self-interest at heart. Dog food manufacturers only put food in bright, shiny packaging for our benefit. Dogs don't care if the biscuits inside are pressed into pretty little bone-shaped pieces of kibble. Have a look at the grain and meat content of these 'best sellers' and ask yourself how 'moist and meaty' can the food really be with only 6% meat content. And if there is only 6% meat and 10% vegetables in there, what on earth makes up the other 84% of the food?

A good place to check the actual content of your dog's food is **www.allaboutdogfood.co.uk.** It also gives some idea as to the provenance of the meat used in the food.

Try to provide the best-quality food you can afford, and don't fall for the hype about the amazing behaviour-changing effects of any one particular food type. Some raw feeders get particularly evangelical about the benefits of feeding raw food, but I have never found raw-fed dogs to be any better behaved than dogs that are fed with any other kind of food. Raw is probably a great choice for some dogs, but it doesn't suit all, and you need to strike a balance between finding a food that is nutritious and that also makes it easy for you to train and entertain your dog.

Be careful not to overfeed your dog either. There is a growing trend of obesity in pets, so take steps to stop your dog from putting on weight. Are you unable to see his waist or feel his ribs anymore? Are his poos so big they look like they have come out of a much larger animal? If yes, then consider reducing the food he eats, and you will no doubt increase his lifespan and the amount of time he will therefore spend with you.

So what you feed your dog is important, but I have found that environmental factors, together with the daily interaction that a dog gets with you, have the greatest impact on a dog's overall behaviour.

Appropriate exercise

Wow, who would have thought it? Dogs need a certain amount of exercise and stimulation *every day*? This may seem a little tedious, but it's surprising how many people neglect their dog's exercise and then act surprised when behaviour problems develop very quickly.

You should know your own dog. If he is bouncing off the walls at 7pm at night and howls like a wolf whenever you leave him alone, then you should probably try exercising him a bit more and providing something to entertain him while he waits for you to come home.

Daily walks are important, but they aren't the be-all and end-all, and there are many quicker, easier, and more effective ways to exercise your dog than taking him for a walk.

Off-leash exercise should be something every dog gets if it's safe to do so, and if you don't or can't provide that at the moment, then you should make it an aim. It's much easier to get rid of a dog's energy when he is off lead or on a long lead. If you don't believe me, then see how far you have to walk a dog to get him as tired as you can by throwing a ball for 10 minutes. If it's less than an hour, I will send you a prize...

How your dog gets his daily exercise is as important as the amount he gets, and if you can be the thing who provides all of your dog's exercise, stimulation, and entertainment, he will be much easier to control.

Interaction

At the start of this chapter, I mentioned about dogs being rather unique creatures in the way they seem to thrive and even crave attention and play. Well, by play I just mean interaction and having fun, and trust me, your dog wants some fun in his life. If you think that play is just something that your dog does with another dog, then you are about to have your eyes well and truly opened. Your dog doesn't really care where he gets his entertainment from, and most dogs will happily play with a human, a dog, a cat, or even a parrot, but who your dog is allowed to play with and sees as fun has a great impact on how he will behave.

There are loads of videos on YouTube showing dogs that have seemingly made friends with cats, birds, and even lions. If you search for Bubbles and Bella Best Friends, you will see a dog playing and interacting with an elephant. Bella even uses Bubbles as a diving board.

Sadly, a lot of our pet dogs get their main interaction and play from searching for and chasing birds or other dogs. Is it any wonder that trips to the park are so stressful?

Myth buster – dogs need to be dogs

Seriously, what the bloody hell does that mean? I hear this a lot, and it's usually said by people who have little or no control over their own dogs. I'm not judging here because I used to have no control over my dogs either, and I also used to use this as an excuse whenever my dog did something that I was embarrassed about.

My dog would run over to play with another dog in the park, and as an excuse to the owner who clearly didn't want me to be there, I would come out with 'It's OK; he just wants to play' or 'He just loves other dogs' when the other owner was probably thinking 'No, actually he's not friendly; he's a bloody nuisance!'

See, being a superhero dog owner isn't just about your dog. It's also about your community. When you walk out of your front door, you are your dog's keeper and the ambassador for responsible dog owners in your town. Some people don't like dogs. They don't care how friendly he is. They don't want your dog near them. If you allow your dog to bother other people, then you are impinging on their freedom. This makes you no better than a fly-tipper or an antisocial neighbour who plays loud music at three in the morning. If that sounds harsh, it's because it's meant to. There are many pleasures that come with owning a dog, but with that pleasure comes great responsibility. And if he's your dog, then he's your responsibility.

Domestic dogs are very much a man-made creature anyway and not wild like a wolf. We have bred dogs to do many different jobs like herding, guarding, retrieving, and yes, even to become lap dogs. You will see as we progress that it's possible for you to influence exactly what your dog needs to be a dog.

Of course, we generalise and say that gun dogs like chasing birds and terriers like to kill stuff, but that's not strictly true, and there are many overlaps between what various breeds of dogs enjoy doing. But most dogs enjoy running, playing, eating, chewing, sniffing, and sleeping in a safe place.

So far that doesn't seem like a terribly exhaustive list of needs for us to satisfy, does it?

Your dog needs to feel safe

More precisely, I mean a safe place to eat, relax, sleep, and exercise. This might sound pretty obvious, but your dog needs a non-threatening environment to live and exercise in, and you should aim to make your dog's life as stress free as possible. This doesn't mean he should have free rein to do whatever he wants. There aren't many more annoying things than a spoilt dog that lacks any kind of self-control, well, except maybe a spoilt child. The structure and routine you provide for your dog will contribute massively to how safe and content he feels.

So does your dog feel safe? Is he ever anxious either at home when he is eating or when you are out walking?

Dogs often won't do normal things when they feel threatened or stressed, and quite often the simple act of removing the stressful element and giving the dog something else to think about instead will do wonders for his well-being.

Barry the Bordeaux barks at our front window when people pass by the house. He is a guarding breed, so this is to be expected, but he does tend to do it more when Beth is home alone with him, and it can get quite annoying after a while. Now as well as teaching him to go to his bed and be quiet, we can also do practical things like lower the blinds or leave him in a different room when we go out.

There are bound to be things your dog does that you could fix very quickly by just changing the routine slightly. If there are, write them down here. Identifying quick wins like this can go a long way to fixing some behaviour issues. When we add these quick wins to some of the more strategic dog training exercises in the coming chapters, we will put your dog training on steroids and supercharge the results you get.

We will be adding lots of useful dog training tools to your kitbox, but it's not all about doing more. Sometimes doing less or doing slightly different things can make a huge change too.

So start now and think of somewhere that makes your dog feel stressed, unsafe, or just plain pissed off. Then write down some of the ways you can help to remove the stressful element from the situation. Then once you have written it down, DO IT and see what happens. The key is in the doing here; it's no good just writing it down. So if your dog's biggest stress is when he sees other dogs on a walk, and you continue to walk him where he always sees them, he will without doubt continue to whine or bark and lunge at them as he always has. This is until you teach him something else to do, that is.

Where does my dog get stressed and display a behaviour that I would like to change?

What can I do TODAY to remove that stress and make life better for us both?

1)

2)

3)

I'm not saying it's easy to change your routine. And finding somewhere to walk your dog where there are no other dogs around is going to require some effort. You may have to get up earlier in the day or drive somewhere quieter. But it can be done, and the pay-off for you and your dog will be almost instant. Yes, your dog may still be a little anxious at first, but he should be quite interested to explore the new surroundings. But you will have removed the distraction that was causing you both so much stress, and you will have created a better learning environment to do some training.

Look, your dog needs a leader in his life. Yes, I said it, and I can hear the positive woo woo dog training gurus crying into their fruit teas now when I mention leader, but let's get real here. Anyone who thinks that you are in a 50/50 relationship with your dog and you can let your dog decide what to do probably shouldn't own one. Dogs are unbelievably smart, but they are still just dogs. Your dog will feel safer and more secure if you take all of the difficult decisions that may get him into trouble completely out of his hands.

Einstein said the definition of insanity is doing the same thing over and over again and expecting a different result. Well, Albert would have made a great dog trainer because that's what dog owners do all the time. You can let your dog off lead in the park again tomorrow, but I will bet you all of the bones in a butcher's shop that he will run away from you as soon as he sees the thing that caused him to run away yesterday, and the day before that.

You need to be your dog's best friend, teacher, and his leader too. There are many different kinds of leaders in the world.

You don't have to be a Stalin or an Idi Amin and rule your dog by fear. You can also be a Gandhi or a Martin Luther King. Leaders are necessary and leaders are also followed. We follow those who inspire us and who we believe in, and we follow not because we have to but because we want to. It really is a beautiful thing to own a dog that follows you and does what you need him to do, not because you force him but because he wants to.

As long as the dog is getting enough exercise and stimulation, then it doesn't really matter what kind of house you have. I don't subscribe to the rather outdated view that you shouldn't own a big dog if you live in a flat. I know people who live very successfully with two or more dogs in apartments, and I have also known dog owners who, despite having lots of land, owned dogs that lived incredibly boring lives and who probably shouldn't have had a dog at all.

It's my experience that dogs need surprisingly little to feel safe and relaxed. A comfy bed in the corner of a room and a safe place to eat where he doesn't feel threatened in any way will suffice. This may mean your dog has to eat alone, away from children or other dogs you own. And of course he needs an exercise routine that provides an outlet for his daily energy build-up.

Please complete the exercise above and identify what if anything is stressing your dog or making him feel like he has to defend himself. Then take steps to remove that thing. You will discover some more strategies for managing the situation better in the coming chapters, but for now let's just identify some big rocks we want to smash.

For what it's worth, I have personally looked after hundreds of dogs of all different breed types in my home, and all have settled in well and felt safe, when I provided a routine that gave them enough exercise, an environment they felt comfortable in, and a warm bed.

But there is one more need that every dog has, and it's one that most dog owners miss out altogether. Think of this as a secret ingredient your dog needs. If you get it right, you will eliminate many of your dog's problems and give him a reason to want to listen to you.

Challenge

In her excellent book *Making Animals Happy,* Temple Grandin talks about an animal having four core blue-ribbon emotions, one of them being a 'SEEKING' mode. She points to research by Dr Jaap Panksepp, who describes the seeking mode as a combination of wanting something really good, looking forward to something really good, and curiosity. I think this pretty much nails how our dogs and all mammals live their daily lives.

So if your dog is looking for things to do, and I have no doubt that he is, then it's our job as the owner to provide the challenge and purpose that your dog is looking for. Later in the book, we will look to give our dogs a job, but for now I would like you to think about providing a series of daily challenges for your dog, which will make him happy and keep him out of mischief.

I call it providing your dog's daily challenges, mainly because I want you to think of this as something that you can provide for your dog. The challenges your dog faces each day will have a huge impact on how much control you have over him and how happy, content, and easy to manage he is.

Dogs have a drive to explore and experience pleasurable events each day, and when confronted with a challenge, they have a real will to win too, especially if the reward is pleasurable for them. Dogs love winning, and you can see examples of their competitive nature in many everyday activities.

Dogs want something to do with their lives, and they will take any opportunity to prove themselves, to get something they perceive as being rewarding. For too many dogs, the challenges they meet on a daily basis don't involve the owner, or certainly not in a good way.

You can see this when two or more dogs are together, and they come across a bush or tree. They will take turns to scent-mark, and each one will walk away thinking he has left his mark. When one of them sees another one mark the tree, he will go back again to redo his mark. What's the big deal you may think? Well, one of the main reasons for pulling on the lead is a dog either following the scent trail of another dog, or wanting to get to the next information-packed pee-stained lamp post. Then once they have repeated that behaviour a few times, it becomes a habit, and before you know it, all your dog is interested in is looking for other dogs' scents. He may progress from lamp posts to wanting to find an actual dog.

So a dog that an owner is finding difficult to manage may have a day that goes like this.

The dog wakes up and has a short walk with his owner. He spends most of the walk pulling on the lead to scent-mark, and when he comes across another dog, he either pulls to get to it or responds by barking. When he gets home, he is fed his bowl of food, which he picks at during the day. The dog enjoys barking at the postman at 10 o'clock, and then at lunchtime, a dog walker comes and takes the dog to a field where he enjoys an energetic hour chasing, playing, mouthing, and wrestling with his doggy friends. He then sleeps until the owner returns, and he has another walk before his tea and then bed.

The dog is undoubtedly getting plenty of exercise, play, and interaction in his day. He also has some challenge in his life too. He finds barking at the postman very exciting, although the postman and the neighbours aren't that keen. Pulling on the lead is another enjoyable activity too. Its urts a little, but it's a physical challenge for him, and the pay-off of being able to smell each new lamp post and then wee on it is well worth the effort of a sore neck. The best part of the dog's day comes at lunchtime when he gets to play with all his doggy friends. He enjoys playing with the other dogs so much that he sees all dogs as potential playmates now. He has become dog reactive, and the barking and lunging he does at strange dogs when he is walking on lead with his owner and the playing with other dogs at the doggy day care are more closely related than you may think. I will come onto that in the next chapter.

So this dog faces many challenges throughout the day that he enjoys, but they will undoubtedly cause a lot of stress for his owner.

But more importantly, what challenges does your dog face on a daily basis, and how many of those challenges are provided by and involve you?

Is your dog dependent on you for fun and entertainment at home AND more importantly when you exercise him? Can you provide a daily routine for your dog that means he is happy and fulfilled and easy to manage? I think you can, and it's your responsibility to do that for your dog. I will help you make some simple changes to your dog's routine that will make your life much easier and more enjoyable.

What does a fulfilling day look like? Well, let's go to the biggest dog show in the world.

I love watching Crufts on the TV each year, but not so much for the judging, which isn't my cup of tea. And as someone who owns a rescue Dogue de Bordeaux with a tooth missing and no tail, I am more interested in how a dog acts than how he looks. But I do love the variety of dogs on display at Crufts. It's just a huge outpouring of doggy love, and you get to see not only lots of unusual breeds but also the different activities that dogs can take part in. There are loads of displays showing off everything from agility to scentwork, obedience, and heelwork to music, as well as gun dog and police dog demonstrations. I just love watching man (or woman) and dog enjoying an activity together.

Anyway, the part that has almost everyone hooked is the friends-for-life section. Here the focus falls on six owners whose dogs have transformed their owners' lives. These are often some kind of assistance dogs that help their owners. Sometimes they are pedigree dogs that have been trained in a special discipline, such as a medical detection dog. But often they are just regular dogs that have helped their owners through tough times in their lives and now fulfil their lives as great companion dogs. And without the high-vis coats that tell you they are assistance dogs, they are just like regular dogs. Well, that's not quite true; they look like really well-behaved, regular dogs. I think if I was going to pick a perfect dog that would make an ideal pet dog for most 21st-century dog owners, I would pick a friends-for-life dog.

Are these friends-for-life dogs well behaved because they have been trained to do assistance work, or would they still be perfect pet dogs if they hadn't had all the training and just entered a normal family where they were just required to be a normal pet dog?

That's an interesting question.

Many of the dogs who go on to provide assistance as guide dogs for blind people are picked as puppies based on their temperament, as are dogs who are required to do specialist service jobs in the police and Army. But there are many service dogs that come from rescue centres and go on to be assistance dogs and provide equally amazing service to those who need it.

The Freedom Service Dogs of America charity only uses rescue dogs that it trains up to help and enhance the lives of people with a variety of disabilities. It carefully selects dogs and only chooses those with no behavioural problems from the shelters.

These are dogs that have been given up on for one reason or another but now have a happy and fulfilling life, doing a job that allows them to have a second chance in a new home and also give something back to the community.

I think without a doubt that the training helps, and as you will see, the more challenge and purpose you can give your dog, the better behaved he will be. But the good behaviour that the assistance dogs display is made up of what they have not been allowed to do, as well as the assistance tricks they have been taught. If we could in some small way copy what these rescue organisations do and teach a dog something new, then we would have a much greater chance of keeping dogs and owners together.

I think the more you can provide your dog with a 'job' to do within your home, the happier he will be and the fewer behaviour problems you will encounter. His job doesn't need to be anything as complicated as detecting when your blood sugar is low either. Your dog's job can just be a series of challenges that make up his daily routine.

I hope you agree that a dog that has a 'why' and a purpose to his life makes what I would consider to be the perfect pet dog. So what kind of challenges can you give your dog, and how exactly can you teach him a new routine?

Chapter summary

- Everyone should know what their dog needs to be happy. It is not an exhaustive list. Any behaviour problems that your dog has will probably be happening because he doesn't feel safe, isn't getting enough exercise and challenge, or is getting the wrong kind of food and interaction in his daily routine. But you can change this quite quickly if you want to.

- Most dog owners forget that their dog needs and wants some fun in his life. There's a reason why when you take him to the park he is more interested in going off to play with another dog than that piece of cheese you are holding. Well, he doesn't want food; he wants to enjoy himself. If you can be the fun thing in his life, then he will choose to be with you instead.

- So can you go from being your dog's chauffeur to his superhero? You bet your butt you can. Before you begin that transformation though, we should probably find out how dogs learn to do things and more importantly how your own dog has learned to do all the annoying things he already does. We will look at this in the next chapter.

CHAPTER 4
HOW DOGS LEARN

"What counts is not necessarily the size of the dog in the fight;
it's the size of the fight in the dog."
– Dwight D Eisenhower

Old Dwight made a very good point with that quote, and if you have ever met a feisty and fearless terrier, you will know exactly what he is talking about. Just like you have, your dog has had to learn everything in his life, and once you know exactly how he learns, you will be much better equipped to teach him something new. Your dog also has breed characteristics that we humans don't share.

My dad, his dad, and his dad before him all worked in the local pit colliery in Seaham, County Durham, but I never followed them down the mine and not just because it was closed either. I don't even look much like my dad. Before we discuss how a dog learns, we should probably take a quick look at how your dog's breed can affect how he behaves.

Almost all pedigree dogs will display some kind of breed characteristics. You know what I mean: Pointers like to point, Dobermans like to guard, and Pugs and Labradors are really greedy. I'm kidding about the last one; well, only a little, but you get the idea.

Herders gonna herd

Most pedigree dogs have been bred over many hundreds of years to do a very specific job, and without much input from us the breed character will come out. For example, imagine if you owned a Pointer and he was exercised quite happily in your garden every day. Then, at six months old you take him to a big field and let him off lead for the first time. He will probably sniff along the grass verge exploring, and then as his confidence grows, he may wander a little further away from you. Now at some point in the next few minutes, I guarantee that he will lift his head and catch the tiniest scent of a pheasant (or another bird), and if you watch closely you will see something magical happen...

Think of the Spider-Man film when he gets bitten by the toxic spider. He goes to bed, and you get this animation of his DNA mutating and changing his whole body, and he's never the same again.

There's an awakening within the dog. His instinct kicks in, and the very reason for his existence as a breed starts to appear. He will sniff the air a few times, and using his spider-sense pointer powers he will lock on to the scent and pinpoint the location of the bird. Then he will very slowly take a couple of steps forward and point.

Now if you are a hunting enthusiast, you would feel quite proud of yourself right now, because you would know your Pointer is into birds. And you could look forward to a time in the future when you have trained him to search for and locate the bird, stand stock-still until you catch up with him, and then be sent forward to flush the quarry for you to shoot.

For most pet dog owners, however, this is usually the moment where they say 'Oh shit!' and wonder how long it will be before they can catch the dog and get him back on lead again.

So that's just one example of how a gun-dog owner may be caught unawares by the power of their dog's breed instinct. But this happens with almost all breeds, and you can explain away the reason why certain dogs do certain things by saying, 'But that's what he is supposed to do.'

For example, a dog owner might say, 'My Beagle wants to sniff every single thing whenever I try and walk him.' Beagles were commonly used to hunt and track a fox over great distances. The fact that he's never seen a fox before is irrelevant. As soon as he steps outside, his instinct is telling him to put his nose on the ground and look for stuff. That's what he's supposed to do.

To illustrate the point still further, I have heard people say the following about their dogs:

'My Rottweiler doesn't like strangers who come to the house.'

'My Lurcher is off like a shot whenever he catches sight of a rabbit.'

'My Terrier destroys every toy I buy him.'

'My Collie stalks and tries to round up other dogs and even people.'

'My Husky pulls really hard on the lead, and when I let him off he can run for hours.'

YES, THAT'S WHAT THEY ARE SUPPOSED TO DO.

So do some research to obtain an understanding of what your breed of dog was created to do. It will help explain why he enjoys doing certain things. The breed characteristics may take a while to come out and in some cases may not show themselves until a dog has matured. This explains why some owners of guarding breeds are often forced to seek out the advice of a dog trainer when their nine-month-old Rottweiler, Doberman, or German Shepherd has started to become aggressive when people approach them or come to their house. Well yeah, he's a guarding breed. That's what he's supposed to do.

Or a breed characteristic may lay dormant until your dog is exposed to a certain situation later in his life.

Here is an example. A terrier that has lived in an urban environment suddenly finds himself on a walk in the countryside with his owner for the first time. They are walking along the lane, and the dog is sniffing in the long grass. He suddenly disturbs a fat mouse who tries to make a run for it. The terrier's instinct kicks in, and the dog's first reaction is to pick up and chomp that mouse. After all, that's what he is supposed to do.

Of course, it's also possible for a breed characteristic to never develop at all. I've met Pointers who couldn't care less if a pheasant was cleaning himself in a bird bath right in front of them. But these are the exceptions to the rule, and you should generally expect your dog to display some of the traits that he has been born with. Generally, the more specialised a job the dog was bred for, the stronger the breed instinct will be.

I also don't want to pigeonhole any particular breed here, because I know Dobermans that are incredibly friendly and welcoming of strangers, and I've also met Pugs and Chihuahuas that are aggressive to anything they meet. But ignore your dog's breed at your peril.

You can, however, put steps in place to ensure that his breed instincts don't take over and make it impossible for you to live with and exercise him.

So if it's within a dog to want do certain things before he's even born, then how do we teach him anything at all? Doesn't the breed instinct win over every time?

The answer is no, and that's because it's not all about the breeding.

There is a way to ensure our dogs still do what we want despite the breed, but to help us find out more, we are going to take a trip into my vegetable garden.

Unfortunately, we don't even own a garden as such. Ours is a Victorian terraced house and so we have a yard with pots… or a yarden if you like.

I do like flowers, but I'm more interested in the stuff we can actually eat like fruit and vegetables, and even in our little yarden we have successfully grown apples, courgettes, berries, and all kinds of beans, but the crop that dominates the annual vegetable challenge is the tomato.

Every year we manage to a greater or a lesser degree to grow some tomatoes, but the results do vary a lot.

Come late summer, we always end up with some kind of crop, but surprisingly it hasn't mattered whether I have grown the plants from expensive organic seeds or just bought some cheap part-grown plants from the garden centre that looked destined for the compost heap.

I grow my plants outside, so the weather plays its part, but I think the thing that makes the biggest difference to how much fruit the plants produce is how consistently I have tended to the plants over the summer. There isn't a lot to it really. You need to make sure they always have enough water, but not too much. Provide a pole so they can grow straight, and pinch out the side shoots that you don't want.

But you have to do this consistently. Let the plants dry out, and they will soon die. Forget to pinch out the side shoots, and you will have too many branches that produce small or no fruit. And with no pole to keep it straight, the plant will eventually fall over.

So like my planting (some grown from seed, some bought as part- or full-grown plants), your dog may have come into your life as a puppy, or from a rescue, or as an older dog.

But regardless of where you got your dog or how old he is, it's what you <u>consistently do with him</u> from now on that will determine how well he grows and develops.

How your dog has learned what to do

I'm not a fan of big words, but when it comes to explaining why your dog does certain things, there are two words you need to know and understand, and they are consequence and association.

If you have ever taught your dog to sit, you will already be aware of consequence and association. But how did you teach him to do it? You may have taught him by pushing his bum down to the floor while you said 'Sit', which works. More likely, you stood with a dog treat and repeated 'Sit' 27 times until your dog eventually did sit, then you gave him the biscuit. You may have lured your dog into a 'sit', in which case, well done you. If you don't know what luring is, don't worry; we will cover that soon. But teaching a dog to sit is pretty easy, isn't it? How has your dog learned to do all the other things in his life? Well, by consequence and association as well.

Imagine for a moment it's high summer and you are enjoying a barbeque in your garden. You have friends round, and cool beers are helping wash down the overcooked sausages and burgers. The next day, your dog heads outside for a toilet break, and he is drawn to the smell around where the barbeque was situated. While he is sniffing in the grass, he comes across a tiny but nevertheless very tasty bit of steak that someone dropped the day before. Bingo, thinks the dog, yum

yum, thank you very much. You call him in, and so he has his wee and comes inside.

For his next toilet break he immediately wanders over to the spot where he found the misplaced meat. And after scrabbling around a bit, he discovers a bit of bacon under a deckchair. Ay caramba, free bacon, yum yum, thank you very much. You start calling him in, and after he does a 'recce' of the whole area, he finally does his toilet and heads back to the house.

Now, dear reader, which part of the garden do you think he will head towards next time he is let out? Yes, the barbeque, you guessed it, hurrah! This time, however, no one is watching the dog, and while there's no food left on the floor, his nose eventually leads him to the grill of the barbeque, which you haven't had time to put away or even clean. But that doesn't matter, because now your dog is standing on his hind legs and is cleaning the grill for you... what a helpful doggy he is. The only slight problem is that for the next two months you are unable to get your dog to come back into the house without bribing him in with treats.

So this is a little story that should neatly explain the principles of consequence and association. The dog began very quickly to associate getting a reward, in this case a very high-value random reward, with just wandering in a certain area of the garden. And the consequence of going to the barbeque area was quickly reinforced with some other tasty finds. And the consequence for you is it is now harder to get him to come back into the house again. But the dog learned that when he went to a particular area of the garden, he was rewarded, so this is still a learned behaviour.

Now if you had a dog that you always struggled to get back in the house when you let him outside, you could reverse-engineer this quite easily. Get something super tasty like a bit of leftover bacon or burger or a bit of cheese from the fridge, if you had nothing handy. Then before you let your dog out of the house, show him the tasty food and place it in his food bowl. Make sure he has seen it, but don't let him eat it – use a lead on him if it's easier. Then lead him outside and wait for him to do his business. When he is done, he is likely to run straight to the back door. Then you can let him in, and he will run straight to the bowl to have his treat. Bingo, we have just taught the dog it's more rewarding to come in than it is to stay out. If your dog isn't food motivated, just use something else he likes instead.

Now here is a slightly different scenario. You let your dog out for a toilet break, and he sniffs around the barbeque and steps on a piece of glass. He isn't hurt too badly thankfully, but he certainly didn't like it, and now he is understandably a bit wary of going to that area of the garden. A few days later, you let him out, and he seems to be forgetting about it, when just as he is about to 'go', some muppet lets a firework off in the adjoining street to yours. Your dog quite literally shits himself and runs into the house with his tail between his legs and stands in the corner of the kitchen shaking. The look on his face tells you in no uncertain terms that he is not going back into that garden any time soon.

You understand the basic premise, I hope. If your dog does something and he gets rewarded, then he is probably going to want to do it again, and if the experience is a bad one, then the dog will avoid it. You and I are not much different.

How many times have you heard a friend say something like, 'I went for a meal at that new Italian place in town. Well, they brought the wrong food, and when it eventually came, it was cold, and the service was shocking all night. I'm never going back there ever again!' A bad experience will lead us to avoid the thing that brought the bad outcome – unless, of course, you like bad service.

So these things are what we call learned behaviour traits. They are actions our dogs take because there are good and bad consequences to them. Almost everything your dog does on a daily basis can be explained as a learned behaviour. You may not have necessarily taught your dog that behaviour; in fact, you probably didn't teach him, but he's learned it anyway, and so he's going to do it.

If you think about it, there should be lots of things your dog does that he associates with pleasure or a pleasurable outcome for him. The trick to training your dog is to find as many things as possible that you can use to reward your dog. Well, I will rephrase that. There are already lots of things your dog likes; you just need to identify them and start pairing those rewards to the actions you want your dog to do, and that's what we will be doing in the next chapter.

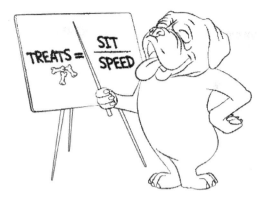

Exercise:

Think of three things your dog does that he associates with a good and bad consequence. Remember he is a dog, so it might not be something that *you* think is pleasurable; it's what your dog likes. What makes his tail wag and what causes it to disappear between his legs? Give this some thought, and remember I'm not looking for actions you have trained your dog to do; rather, I would like you to write down things he does, because by luck or happy accident he has found them to be pleasurable, or not.

For example, when Sid was a puppy and he was parading around the living room with a sock in his mouth, he accidentally stood in a hot cup of coffee. No real harm was done, but now he avoids any cups on the floor like they are radioactive. He will move away from you when pick your cup up too.

Three things my dog has learned to associate with a good consequence:

1)

2)

3)

Three things my dog has learned to associate with a bad experience:

1)

2)

3)

As we progress, you should be developing a better understanding of how dogs learn and more importantly why *your dog* does the things he does. The reason your dog doesn't come back to you may be a different reason to why someone else's dog doesn't. This isn't a theory book. It's an action plan, and if you take action and do the exercises, then you will get the best results.

We need to identify why our dogs do certain things so we can avoid those things if they are bad, or encourage them if it's something we want the dog to do. This brings us to a fundamental truth that as a dog owner you need to be aware of: your dog is always learning.

Why your dog is always learning

Your dog can learn to pull on the lead. He can learn to jump up at people when he greets them. He can learn to whine or bark or chew your possessions when you go to work and leave him alone. He can learn that going to the park means he gets to play with his doggy friends. Whatever your dog does is going to be either a learned behaviour or a breed trait. So your Collie enjoys running round and round people and other dogs when you go to the park. That's a breed trait and what he is supposed to do. But if he also chases buses and cars, well, that's a learned behaviour. He has learned to chase things that move because that's what he's supposed to do, but he hasn't been given an outlet for his breed instinct. Teaching the Collie to enjoy retrieving a ball or Frisbee would have prevented the bus-chasing problem from occurring.

So which wins in the end, breed trait or learned behaviour?

If the domestication of dogs over the last 200 years has taught us anything, it's that dogs are very trainable. You can train a dog to go against his breed instincts, and you see proof of this all the time. What good would a Labrador be as a guide dog if he pulled his owner over every time a fat pigeon flew overhead? I see a lot of dog owners use the breed as an excuse for a dog behaving badly and just accept that's what their dog will do forever.

But for every owner out there who says that Beagles will always run away, I could show you a perfectly trained one that comes back when called. And the same for terriers that kill things or guard dogs that bark and so on.

The truth is you can train a dog to do just about anything, and as we have already said, you really should train him because he is going to learn to do stuff anyway. And yes, some dogs are way smarter than others, but no matter what breed you own, you should be able to train your dog to do most of the basic stuff I cover in the coming chapters.

Owners of older pedigree dogs should have a good idea by now of what breed traits their dog displays regularly, or doesn't as the case may be. Those of you with puppies need to be aware of your dog's breed characteristics so you can take preventative action and teach a behaviour trait to counteract the breed trait. For example, if you own a guarding breed, then you want to make sure that he is well socialised as a puppy with people, especially men. And if you own any kind of working dog, then you should make sure he is taught that playing a game with you is more enjoyable than rounding up sheep, chasing rabbits, or pointing at pheasants.

So be aware of your own dog's breed traits; they are always going to be there lurking beneath the surface like a crocodile in a swamp, and they may show themselves at any time. But does it matter whether the thing your dog does is a learned behaviour or a breed trait? No, not really, it just helps you understand why he does it. But if he rips up cushions just because he is a terrier, or because he taught himself to do that when you left him home alone, what the heck are you going to do about it now? Well, to misquote Yoda, your dog can't just 'unlearn what he has learned'; you need to teach him something else to do instead.

Back to school

Learning is hard, isn't it? You have to concentrate, read loads of stuff, and copy things out lots of times, and then you have to do it again and again, and it is really boring and makes you tired, doesn't it?

Well, no, not really. At least, it doesn't have to be hard, boring, and tiring. Learning can be fun and exciting, and when it is enjoyable then we learn a hell of a lot faster. Not only that, often we can't wait for the next lesson either. And so it is with dogs too. If you want to teach your dog something new that you want him to do well, then you better bloody well make sure he enjoys doing it. Everything you teach your dog from now on you need to make fun.

Another thing you must take into consideration is the learning environment. When you were a teenager you could probably still do your homework if you had some music playing in the background. But trying to learn your French verbs and play a computer game at the same time would be more difficult. If your friends were playing Twister in the middle of your bedroom while you were studying, you would no doubt find it impossible to concentrate. Your dog will learn something new much faster if he has all the distractions removed too. So don't go to the park and expect your dog to want to do a trick for you, when all his friends are romping merrily in full view of him. That's way too difficult, and you are setting yourself and your dog up for failure.

If possible you should try and avoid or remove any of the things that distract your dog. This isn't as hard as you think, and in the next chapter I will give you an easy-to-follow programme that will help. But removing the distraction while you teach something new will make it much easier for your dog to learn. You will find the learning more enjoyable too, and avoiding the thing that was causing your dog to bark or run away will also mean that bad behaviour traits will fade over time too.

Don't feel the need to test yourself or your dog. For now, just find somewhere quiet and distraction-free to play and have some fun.

From now on, you should try and think how you can make any training or game playing with your dog as much fun as possible. A dog who does drug work in an airport isn't given a series of lectures on the dangers of drugs to society before he starts work each morning. He doesn't give a shit about that; all he cares about is what's in it for him.

So first he is played with a lot, usually with a ball or a tuggy toy. Then over time he is taught to associate locating the scent of the drugs with getting the toy and playing the game. Yes, finding the drugs or explosives is important, but to the dog the toy and the playing come first. They have to, otherwise why would the dog do it? You should approach anything you want to teach your dog the same way.

This is how we are going to progress in the next chapter. You are going to find out the thing your dog loves above all else. This thing will help you to play with, train, and control your dog. Remember dogs are selfish and they like having fun. So if you use items that your dog already likes, then it will be much easier for you to influence him.

Chapter summary

◎ So how your dog behaves comes down to his breed characteristics and the experiences he has had since he was born. Think of it like a computer: the breed characteristics are the hardware that he comes pre-programmed with, and everything he has learned since birth is the software that you add. You are in control of everything your dog learns, and he is always learning, so you need to play an active role in what you allow your dog to learn to enjoy.

◎ Dogs learn by doing. If they do something and they enjoy the experience, then there's a high chance they will want to do it again. Now you know this, you can take steps to ensure that all the fun stuff in your dog's life comes through you. It's your job to make the learning as fun as possible. Identifying and then not allowing your dog to do the things that are fun for him but annoy you is part of the process too. You should fill in the blanks to the questions throughout the book, and this will give you greater clarity in the areas you want to improve on.

◎ Distractions are a bugger. As I write this chapter summary, my mind is wandering, and I'm thinking about what's for tea or if it has stopped raining outside. If I allow myself to be distracted by emails, Facebook, television, or noises in the front street, I will never finish this page, never mind the book. So I turn off my internet, and I lock myself away in a quiet room with no distractions. Yes, my mind may still wander, but I have fewer annoying distractions competing for my attention. I set myself up to succeed. What can you do to keep distractions to a minimum and make it as easy as possible for your dog to succeed?

CHAPTER 5
THE DOG AUDIT

"I never learn anything talking. I only learn things when I ask questions."
– Lou Holtz

In Zen Buddhism, there is a concept called Shoshin. Shoshin is one of the highest states of learning and is otherwise known as 'The Beginner's Mind'. It's where you approach any kind of task in an open and eager way, but with no preconceptions of how the task will be carried out. You can apply this kind of thinking to any problem you come up against in your personal life, business, and also in dog training,

Now before you think I am getting all woo woo on you, let me explain.

Before we start trying to train our dog, wouldn't it make sense to get a connection and bond with him first? To do that it would be helpful if we know what floats their boat. Remember our dogs are selfish and they like doing stuff they like doing, so if we can find out what they like, then we can use that information to motivate them to want to do stuff with us. Does that make sense?

You should be nodding your head, but I understand if you aren't. There are two replies I usually get now.

One is: 'I know what my dog likes! He likes cuddles, tennis balls, and Dairylea chunks.' I will then say, 'Well done! You have already made a start. Now read on and you will find out how to use that information to better influence your dog.'

The second and usually bigger group of people tend to look rather confused and say something like, 'I haven't got a bloody clue, Dom. I know he likes the Labrador next door and he plays every day and he also enjoys taking my sandwiches from me, but apart from that I haven't got a Scooby-Doo.' If that's you, then also don't worry. I was like you too, and like me, you are going to have a lot of fun finding out what your dog likes. By the end of this section you will know exactly what your dog likes and how you can use it to motivate him to do what you want.

Why bother finding out at all? Why not just tell him what we want him to do? Well, you could do that, but I'm guessing that you have been telling your dog to do stuff for quite a while and that hasn't worked out very well so far, has it? I also know that there are some things in your dog's life that he really enjoys doing which don't involve you, and this is where most of your problems come from. It's time for a different approach.

There is another reason you should try and identify what your dog likes – it's what the best dog trainers and behaviourists do. I learned this on a John Rogerson course. Seriously, John knows more about dogs than most of us will ever know. So never assume that you know exactly what your dog likes. You have preconceived ideas based on what you think your dog likes.

It's OK not to know what your dog likes. I can't speak for the ladies, but I know most men, including me, experience this every December when Christmas is fast approaching and we don't know what present to buy our dear wives. It doesn't matter if she has been dropping hints all year; we weren't listening. And we can't just come out and ask her what she wants because she wants to be surprised. Well, you will be pleased to know the similarity ends here because you can ask your dog what he wants.

Now you could, of course, train your dog using a clicker or a whistle (both of which work by the way) and reward him with training treats or anything else that *you want*, but where's the fun in that for your dog? I've had a few jobs in my life, and the best bosses always knew which buttons to press to get me to do something. A sneaky morning off work to go and see one of my kids in a Christmas play was worth more than any bonus to me, and I was more willing to do extra if the reward was right.

Too many people approach dog training with a 'tell tell' attitude to the dog, and the routine for training goes something like this.

'OK dog, come on now, fun's over; we are going to do some training. OK.' *Stern face – deep voice* – 'Dog sit'… 'Sit'… 'Sit please'… 'Doggy sit'… 'Sit!'… *Repeat the command five or six times, getting slightly louder each time* – Dog eventually sits and is chucked a treat. Great job, you think to yourself. But goodness it took a bit longer than I wanted it to. It's as if he doesn't understand what I want him to do.

Wow, thinks the dog, that was a pleasant experience. I can't wait for my next training session. NOT!

When we approach dog training like a strict Dickensian boarding school headmaster, is it any wonder that our dogs would rather bugger off and play with another dog or chase squirrels when we take them to the park than do a 'sit' with us with nothing but a packet of crusty old training treats?

Remember our dogs are selfish and they like doing stuff they enjoy, so let's find out what they enjoy and use that to train them. This is the easiest, fairest, and most fun way to connect and bond with and train your dog, in my opinion.

Finding this out is going to help you not to get yourself in sticky situations with your dog too. You will know when it is a good time to let him off lead or not. The more things your dog enjoys that you can control, the easier it will be to get him to do what you want him to do. This exercise will transform you from being a mere mortal dog owner to your dog's superhero. And I call this 'Finding the Kryptonite'.

What is the canine Kryptonite?

The Kryptonite is the thing (or things) that turn your dog from a sleepy hound into a fun-loving mega mutt. It will give you special powers over your dog and allow you to play with and control him in a way you may never have thought possible before now.

Before we dive into the full (super) dog audit, I have another exercise for you.

I would like you to put the book to one side and mentally walk a day in your dog's paws, from the moment he wakes up to the time you tuck him up in bed. What experiences during his day excite him and make his tail wag? What gets him barking and jumping up and down with glee? What does he crave? Does he carry anything around or protect anything? What does he like eating and begging from you, and what makes him drool with anticipation? What places does he like going to? What makes him spin round and round? Does he ever wet himself with excitement? What do you think gives your dog that Christmas-morning feeling?

Now put this book to one side and have a little think... And remember we are looking for the things that HE likes doing, not what you like him to do. List below the five things that get your dog really excited in his day:

1)

2)

3)

4)

5)

So how did you get on? Were they what you thought they were going to be?

See, the Kryptonite may not be the thing you think it is, and it also may not be the thing you want it to be either, but find it we must, because once you know, it's going to be much easier to motivate your dog to love being with you and do what you want.

Your dog's Kryptonite will fall into two categories.

It will be something like a ball or a stick, but it could be a hairbrush, a plastic bottle, or a blanket. I've had people tell me their dogs love socks, ice cream, and tangerines. Barry my Dogue de Bordeaux's favourite thing is Yorkshire puddings. The Kryptonite is something that **you** can control pretty easily. By control I mean hold it in your hand and carry it around with you and remove it from your dog when you need to.

The second category is things that excite and motivate your dog that you can't control as easily, like maybe eating discarded pizza or pasties in the park or barking at the TV. It may well be playing with other dogs or chasing birds or cats, pheasants or the postman, people on bicycles or even running after aeroplane trails.

If your dog's Kryptonite is something in the second group, then we are going to get your dog more interested in something you can control. There will be one dog in a hundred who isn't really interested in anything at all. The dog that just plods his way through life, is quite happy minding his own business, and never bothers anyone else. If that's your dog, then well done, he's perfect, so just enjoy him as he is. However, if your dog is interested in things, but they don't involve you, then you just need to work harder.

Please do not worry if you can't think of anything your dog likes that you can control. It's out there and we will find it. I have had people tell me that their dog only likes playing with other dogs, but by playing with other dogs, your dog is telling you he is, in effect, 'playful'. We just need you to be as playful as another dog. But how can I be as playful as another dog, I hear you say?

Well, you can, and you will 'be more dog', and your dog will want to be with you more than anything else.

I'm not saying it's easy to do this. It can be difficult for some pet dog owners, especially when their dog's Kryptonite is another dog. If your dog loves playing with other dogs or chasing birds, then you are at the mercy of every dog or bird that ever shows up when you are out walking.

Yes, you could technically reward your dog for coming back, by letting him go and play with other dogs. However, remember I'm all for making things as easy as possible for you, so we are going to concentrate on getting your dog interested in things that YOU can control quickly and easily, which in turn will enable you to keep your dog with you even when there are other distractions around.

In chapter 3 we covered the basic needs of a dog and that included interaction and play. Your dog is going to enjoy something in his life, so wouldn't it be nice if it was you?

The magic feather

I have a little story for you, particularly if you are still unsure about the whole canine Kryptonite thing. This may convince you that it's worth investing your time in playing with your dog so you can find the thing or things that are going to help you connect, bond, and play with him, and train him.

The summer of 2013 was a good one; business was good and the sun was out almost every day. This was especially enjoyable for us dog walkers, as it meant shorts, T-shirts, sunglasses, and sunblock instead of wellies, Barbours, and woolly hats, but it presented some challenges with the dogs. The main one was how to keep them cool. It probably won't surprise you to know that most of our clients like their dogs to be walked around at lunchtime as this is slap bang in the middle of the time they are out of the house at work. This is also the warmest part of the day. Now being in the North East of England, this isn't usually a problem, but this was the warmest, driest summer for several years, so it was not the ideal time of the day to be exercising any dog.

Fortunately, in Sunderland we are blessed with many beautiful beaches, and we generally spend a lot of time playing with and training the dogs there. We also have a lot of dogs who love the water too, and this year I had set myself a challenge to teach all the dogs to swim that couldn't already. I'm a firm believer in getting hands-on with all my dog training, and so I knew the best way for me to help the dogs to swim was to get in the water with them. However, even in a hot summer, the sea is pretty cold here, so we found a nice quiet man-made lake that I could easily spend a bit of time in without my lily-white legs turning blue.

We had a lot of fun that summer and successfully managed to get almost all of the dogs to enjoy swimming, or at least to feel more comfortable in the water. I say almost, because there were a few that either weren't very keen or were just not really suited to swimming, like Nell the Samoyed, who has a very thick and heavy coat.

One summer's day we arrived at our usual spot at the lake and started to play with the dogs, and this is the day when the penny dropped for me about how powerful a dog's Kryptonite can be. The area near to where we were playing in the water had evidently been privy to some kind of fox attack on a swan the previous day, and one of our party, little Stuey the Pug, was taking a very keen interest in the scene of the swan massacre, which was now strewn with swan feathers. Now Stuey the Pug is a lovely little guy that is always a pleasure to walk. He isn't much into playing with toys, but he always stays close by us unless we go in the water. He isn't very keen on swimming, despite our previous efforts.

Today he was Chief Inspector Stu, and try as I might, I couldn't get him to come away from the crime scene. I tried treats and toys but to no avail. Even when we moved further round the lake, he kept trying to head back to the same spot. So just when I thought, 'That's it; he's going to have to go on lead today', I remembered the words of my good friend and dog training mentor, David Davies: *'To get a dog's attention you need to be able to reward him with something that he is interested in at the time.'*

OK then, I thought; if Stuey wants a feather, then Stuey can have a feather. But he will have to follow me to get it.

Would this work? I wasn't really sure to be honest, and my assistant looked at me like I was a little mad. I went and found the biggest (and cleanest) swan feather I could and got Stuey's attention with it. This wasn't too difficult. Then I played with him with the feather, and I teased him a little just the same way I would with a normal dog toy. By now Stuey was very interested in the feather, so much so I was able to back away from him, and he followed me.

Using the feather, I managed to lure him back to where the others were, and I have to admit I was feeling rather pleased. I then began to wonder what I could get Stuey to do for this feather. Well, I was already wet, so I began to edge my way into the lake slowly. And Stuey followed. He was a bit tentative at first, but he took a step or two into the water. I continued to go deeper, and whenever Stuey looked like he was losing interest, I would wave the feather around and let him have a sniff or a little bite of the feather. I went deeper until the water was now up above my knees, and Stuey was almost fully submerged. This was it. I moved back further still so the water rose up to my waist, and lo and behold, that little pug pushed off and started swimming towards me, freestyle.

Well, needless to say, I couldn't believe it, and I'm not sure Stuey could either. He swam for a few minutes, and we repeated this exercise a few more times using the feather as the temporary Kryptonite at the time.

So this little story is a favourite of mine, because it shows you what it's possible to achieve when you find and use your dog's Kryptonite correctly. If I was able to get a pug to swim willingly into a lake even though he doesn't really like swimming, then surely you can get your dog to do what you want by using rewards that he enjoys.

The reward element of dog training is so important. Don't just assume you know what your dog likes.

So now it's time for you to go and find your dog's Kryptonite. This is where we drill down and discover the finer details of what makes your four-legged friend tick. And we are quite literally going to get down too, on the floor that is, so we can test our mutts and see what they enjoy.

Please don't rush the next chapter because you feel you need to get on and 'train your dog' quickly. There are a thousand videos on YouTube showing you how to train a dog, and any numpty can hold a chicken leg in his hand, wait for his dog to sit down and then throw him the food and say he has taught a 'sit'.

What you are going to achieve is something far more sophisticated and worthwhile. At the end of this process, you will truly understand what your dog likes, and then you will be able to use that information to motivate your dog so he actually WANTS to do things for you and enjoys doing them too!

Don't worry if you can't find very many things your dog likes that you can control, or if he doesn't seem interested enough in them to want to play with them with you.

This takes time. Your dog doesn't know how interesting you are yet, so you need to show him. Once you have found your dog's Kryptonite, it's very important that you only allow your dog to see or have it when you are playing with it **with him**. This will make the Kryptonite more special to your dog, and the more you enjoy yourself playing with your dog, the more he will too.

Chapter summary

◉ You may think you have a pretty good idea already what your dog likes and doesn't like. If that's the case, then well done. However, you will be doing me (and your dog) a favour if you do the audit anyway. Getting on the floor and messing about with your dog is great fun, and you will be much better equipped to train your dog once you know what makes him tick.

◉ You can't train your dog until you have his attention, and it is easier to get his attention when you have something he actually likes. So the Kryptonite gives you an easy 'in' to connect with your dog. It's like that first date with your future spouse, when they told you that they also liked Star Trek or rambling or whatever it is that you both now like doing together. Finding the Kryptonite isn't the be-all and end-all, but it's a great place to start if you have never done much training.

◉ Remember this is how the dog trainers do it, and if you want to improve your dog's behaviour, then you need to be his trainer now. I'm not saying you need to join the Kennel Club trainers' scheme or get a degree in canine psychology (unless you want to), but you don't need to qualify for the Olympics to be an athlete either. Buy some trainers and go for a jog, and boom, you're a runner! It's the same with dog training, and anyway, I can't think of anyone better to train your dog than you.

CHAPTER 6
FINDING THE KRYPTONITE

'Control the toy, control the dog'
– John Rogerson

I remember the first time I saw anyone approach training a dog by actually asking the dog what he liked. I was attending a seven-day dog behaviour course with John Rogerson, who is widely regarded as the forefather of modern dog training. The course involved a lot of listening but also lots of opportunities to get hands-on with a dog too. We were housed in a learning centre that was part of the Darlington Dogs Trust rehoming centre, and so we had access to some of the dogs that were there awaiting a new home.

The first dog was brought in, and John proceeded to ask the dog a series of questions, but not in 'Parkinson' style. He offered the dog a series of tests, and he was quickly able to gather a lot of information about the dog. For example, he fed the dog a biscuit, and because the dog took the biscuit very gently, you could reasonably assume that the dog had been fed by humans and maybe even children. He showed him another dog across the room, and when he whined to get to him, it appeared fairly obvious that the dog had maybe lived with another dog or certainly had access to other dogs. This went on for some time until we were able to build a fairly accurate picture of what type of things this particular dog had learned to do in his life. For more information on exactly how John does this, you should check out his excellent book, *The Dog Vinci Code*.

I subsequently learned this is how a lot of trainers and behaviourists assess a dog, the good ones anyway. My friend and colleague David Davies, also a dog trainer, sends a questionnaire to the dog owners, and from the answers, he will have a pretty good idea of why they may be having a certain kind of problem with their dog.

There are many tests you can give a dog, but I have tried to narrow it down to the bare minimum you should do to help you solve the problems you are having with your own dog.

We have been gradually gathering some very basic information about your dog, but now it's time to deep dive into this and find the Kryptonite. These tests are easy, and they are fun, and they are exactly what I drove straight home and did with my own dogs as soon as the course ended that day.

I have split the audit up into five sections, but you can add more categories if you wish.

The information we are looking to gather straightaway is as follows:

- ◉ Your dog's five favourite foods – out of everything he ever eats.
- ◉ Your dog's five favourite toys – or things he likes playing with. This should include stuff you don't like

him playing with, but it's still safe to use, e.g. hairbrushes and slippers.

- ◎ Your dog's five favourite touch points – where he loves being stroked, touched, or tickled.
- ◎ Your dog's five favourite locations – where are the places he goes that get him really excited? Rank them in order.
- ◎ Your dog's five favourite people – should be pretty obvious, but we are going to find out and again rank them in order.

There are two reasons why completing the dog audit will act as a successful kick-starter for all the training that follows.

The first is the information you are going to gather. Knowing what makes your dog's tail wag is very powerful information that we are going to leverage to get him interested in us. Once you have completed this, you will know what and who he likes and loves, but also where he is most distracted and shows his bad behaviour. You can then avoid these places, which will make the playing and the training much easier.

The second reason is the process you go through to find that information requires you to get on the floor and interact with your dog. This is the part many people are afraid of and think, 'What if my... doesn't like me?' My advice is JFDI (just *flipping do it – or insert appropriate swear word *here).

Look, you now know why your dog does the bad things he currently does, and you know he can't unlearn them, so it's your job to teach him something new instead. I promise you this process will be fun, so let's do it. I say again: take your time and enjoy the process.

How do we find out what your dog likes? Quite simply, we ask him. We don't actually say, 'Oi Fido, what do you prefer, gravy bones or hot dogs?' Well, unless you are a dog whisperer and magically know through your Jedi mind tricks what he likes. For the rest of us mere mortals who have to use actual teachable training methods, we are going to ask our dogs another way.

We do this though trial and error and by seeing what he likes. We basically put something in front of him and observe how he reacts to it. Then we see if we can get him more interested in it by playing with it, and once he is wagging his tail, we get something else out and see which one he prefers.

That's a very brief overview, of course, and I am going to show you in much greater detail now how to go through the dog audit step by step.

Setting the scene

Before we begin, I want you to clear the room of any distractions. Remove any KONGS and toys and put any chews away. Then turn the TV off, put some music on that makes you feel happy (keep it fairly low volume though because you want your dog to be able to hear you talk). You should even lower the blinds or close the curtains if you feel a bit self-conscious about anyone peeping in and seeing you play the canine version of The Generation Game...

Then we can begin.

We are going to start with toys and touch and leave food till last. Why? Because food is obvious, and most dogs are interested in food, so please challenge yourself a bit and go with toys first.

I love playing with toys with my dogs. By far the biggest revelation for me since I started my training and adventure business is just how much dogs love playing with toys with humans. You can get quite physical with a dog playing tuggy, and it's much easier to wear a dog out playing a retrieve game than it is walking or running with them. And remember dogs love a *challenge*. Dogs are strong, and they have powerful jaws they enjoy using. Dogs aren't allowed to put their teeth on human skin or our furniture, so it's good if you can provide a challenge that actually allows your dog to use his teeth in a controlled way.

But don't stress if you think your dog doesn't like toys as we are going to use food in a minute. Just have a go with toys anyway; you may surprise yourself.

Start by getting out what you think your dog's most desirable and pleasurable things are. Remember this may not be a traditional dog toy; we are just looking for the thing or things that he loves holding. We can get him to interact with hairbrushes, socks, slippers, plastic bottles, towels, or anything that's safe and usable.

Put your five or six things on a table so your dog can't get the ones you aren't using, and get on the floor and PLAY.

Whoa there, Dom, did you say 'play'? What do you mean 'play'?

I mean play. OK, think of it more as interacting if playing is too much for your cold heart to handle at the moment. I'm just kidding… a little. Seriously, you need to P-L-A-Y. Why do you think we are doing this in the safety of our own homes with the curtains drawn so no one can see us making a fool of ourselves?

What makes your dog tick?

Try and remember what it felt like to play when you were five years old. Yes, it was a long time ago, wasn't it, but life was good, and you had next to nothing to worry about except which biscuit to eat, TV programme to watch, or game to play. Carefree times pretending to be Spider-Man or Wonder Woman and rolling around building forts and playing armies or doctors and nurses. This is what I'm after here, and it's what your dog is after too. It bears repeating, but your dog wants some fun in his life. He probably already has fun, but it just doesn't involve you. Well, you are going to show this dog just how bloody fun you can be!

Toys

Toy exercise:

Get on the floor with a toy (or something he loves), and get his attention with it. By get his attention, I don't mean shove it in his face and say 'LOOK HERE, I HAVE FUN, PLAY NOW.' No, we are going to be a bit subtler than that.

We know that dogs almost always want stuff other people have, so if your dog isn't immediately interested in you, then you can tease your dog just a little. So in a nice cheery voice, you can say something like 'Oooh what's this I've got? Isn't this the most interesting and best slipper ever?' (Or whatever the thing is he likes). Then try and tempt your dog over to you with it. If you read and understood the previous part of this chapter, you will hopefully be using something you know your dog likes, so it shouldn't be too hard to get him to take some notice of you. You have something he wants after all.

Don't get disheartened if he doesn't jump up straightaway; you will have to put in a bit of effort and encourage him. Try and get a bit of interaction going with the toy, but don't be tempted to just give it to him. The idea is you are teaching him to like you and like doing stuff with you because you have stuff he likes. Eventually it won't matter what toy you use, but for now use his favourite things and make things easy for yourself.

So now you have his attention, you can show him the 'Kryptonite'. Let him have a sniff of it, talk to him, and make him feel special.

Next, put that Kryptonite away, get one of the other items, and repeat the same thing. If you are on a roll with your dog, then by all means have more of a play with him, but keep switching between items.

You aren't actually playing with your dog at the moment. All you are looking for is your dog taking an interest in you and showing a desire to have the thing you have. If it's any consolation, your dog may feel a bit awkward too and may not know what to think of this new you. He may be thinking something like, 'Well, this is a new one, isn't it? She's never done this before' or, 'What can she be after?... 'Hmm, hang on though; she has that hairbrush I really like, so I better go and check it out. You never know, she might give it to me, and that would make me very happy indeed.' (And make sure you do a silly dog voice when you read that part too!)

So it's going to take a bit of time, but stick with it. Do the same thing with the second toy you brought, and progress all the way down to your fifth and final item.

By now, you will have an idea of which ones he likes best, so pick up two of the toys your dog was least interested in and repeat the playing game. Which one does your dog like the best? Which is he looking at, and which one does he sniff and nudge you to get at? Put them both on the floor, and see which one he picks up first. The toy he is interested in will be number four on your list, and the one he left on the floor is number five. Do the same things with the others until you can make a list in order of your dog's favourite items of interaction. AKA toys!

My dog's five favourite toys:

1)

2)

3)

4)

5)

The order may change slightly as you go through the audit, but don't worry about that; just take your time and enjoy the process. This isn't just an exercise to do once; practise it a couple of times over a few days, and observe your dog all the time. Is he looking at you ever or always the toy? Does he try and get it off you by sitting or barking or giving you his paw? Can you make something from the bottom of the list more desirable by changing the tone of your voice? If you go squeaky, does he get more excited? Even after a short while playing this, something will become apparent, and that is it's not about the toy; it's what we do with it that matters.

Remember though – information doesn't equal transformation; action does! You are not going to get your dog to love you any more or want to be with you by reading and thinking about it, so have some fun playing with your dog and practise playing with your dog.

So you have officially begun your dog audit, and already you have a very clear idea of the type of toys your dog likes playing with. Well done.

Touch

So while we have our dog's attention, we are going to build on this and continue finding out where our dog likes to be touched and stroked. Why is this important? Well, lots of reasons. Stroking and grooming can be your dog's daily health check. You can check for cuts, bruises, or any lumps he may have, but mainly it's because our dogs enjoy it, and it's good for us too. Stroking a dog has been medically proven to reduce heart rate and stress, so do it daily and consider it a reward to yourself and an important part of your daily routine, just like having a meal with your family or doing some exercise.

So touching and stroking your dog is not only good for you, but he should enjoy it as well. Maybe not so much at first, but the more you do it, the more pleasurable he will find it. And it will also help with your training too. What if having his butt scratched was one of your dog's top three things in the world. Wouldn't you like to know that information so you could use it? You betcha you would, so let's do it. You are probably best doing this exercise after a walk so your dog has less energy and the stroking doesn't get him so excited that he starts jumping all over you. Or you can do as I just suggested and start the affection section after you have done the toy audit.

Exercise:

Start by talking to your dog and give him a stroke on his head. Then move down his back and try his ears next. Which area does he lean into and close his eyes with pleasure? He may even offer a little blissful groan. That's your number one on the list. Now just go round his body slowly and talk to him and see where you think the other four places are. To rank them in order of pleasure, you could try stroking and talking to him in one position and see how long it takes him to get bored. Then start somewhere else. There's no real science to this; it's mainly trial and error. Once again your dog may be thinking 'What's this all about then? This only normally happens on a Saturday evening.'

Your success with this task will depend in part on how much your dog was handled as a puppy. Dogs that have enjoyed being stroked as a puppy will enjoy this more. Some dogs are less keen to be touched in certain places, and certainly the feet, ears, and bum can be areas your dog may feel uncomfortable with you touching. That's why it's important to take your time and talk to your dog. Don't force yourself on him. You want to know what he enjoys and loves, so listen to him, and that means avoid anything that makes him uncomfortable for now.

Repeat this exercise a couple of times, and then rank the top five places your dog likes to be touched in order.

My dog's five favourite touch points:

1)

2)

3)

4)

5)

Now we can move onto food, yummy yummy.

Food

Food is great. I love it and so do my dogs, but if we are being honest, we kind of know our dogs like food, so that's why we do toys and touch first. Also, what happens if you just train your dog with food, and one day in the park you shout at him to come back and he isn't hungry? That's the thing with just using food to train your dog; it can make you lazy. You can lose some of the connection with your dog and just end up becoming a treat dispenser for him. Remember; when using food, we want just as much animation as we did with the toys, so really try and make the food come alive. Remember your dog is quite selfish, and he likes stuff other people are enjoying, so you should make a big fuss of the food, especially when you are using the lower-value treats.

Exercise:

Get your five or six different treats and see which one he likes best. I would suggest putting a very small amount into five cups or bowls and taking each one out in turn. This game is somewhat easier as the dogs are generally more motivated, but you still need to have that conversation with your dog where you say 'Oh, what's this! Look what have I got here, a piece of cheese and a piece of ham. Which one do you like best, my lovely little doggy?' Then take one of each type of food and cup in each hand, put them both under his nose, separate your hands, and see which one his nose follows. Repeat four or five times.

Remember the point of the audit is for you to find five options for each section in a minute, but your training won't be as effective if you just guess. You may be able to tell me after thinking about it for a minute that your dog's top thing in each list is a tennis ball, being stroked behind his ears, and liver treats, but that's not really the point. I want you to get to know your dog a little deeper than that. Once we have all the knowledge, then playing and training become so much easier, so let's get all the tools we need first.

Gradually work your way through the rest of the foodstuffs until you have a list of the ones he liked in order of preference.

My dog's favourite foods:

1)

2)

3)

4)

5)

People

Next we want to find out your dog's five favourite people. Obviously if you live alone with your dog, I'm not suggesting you get married and adopt three children just to do this exercise. Although don't let me stop you either.

No, this is more if you have a family or a regular circle of friends your dog usually sees. The easiest way to see which family member your dog likes would be for you all to go off to the park, where one of you holds the dog on his lead while the others walk a short distance away. Then you let go of the lead while they all encourage the dog to come towards them. The one the dog goes to is the one he likes best. Don't get upset with me if when you try this it wasn't you your dog went to; the dog won't lie.

If the park is too distracting for your dog at the moment, then do the exercise in the house or garden. But don't use food or toys to tempt him in this exercise. We want to know which person he actually likes.

My dog's favourite people:

1)

2)

3)

4)

5)

Places

Next we have the five most stimulating places you take your dog. I'm not suggesting you both go and drive around your town jumping in and out of the car at various locations, so this is one section you can probably do from the comfort of your own chair. However, depending on how well travelled your dog is, you may have a list that is longer than five.

Think about all the places you take your dog and how much he enjoys each place. I would like you to rank these starting with the place where your dog is most excitable and you have the least control over him. You can go into more detail here too because there will be environmental factors that will change things; for example, the list may look like this:

1) Wherever we are when he sees another dog
2) The beach when the tide is out
3) Grandma's house when all the nephews and nieces are there
4) The woods when the pheasants are out

5) When we walk past the scrap yard and he barks at that Doberman he doesn't like

You get the idea.

Now if you went on down the list of every location your dog has ever been to, then after a few hours you would hopefully end up with your sitting room, living room, or elsewhere in your house at the end because your house is likely to be the least stimulating. It's where he spends most of his resting time, and apart from his toys, he has long ago finished being interested in any of the items in the room.

This is convenient for you because this is exactly where you are going to start playing with and training your dog.

What to play with and how to play with your dog

Up to now I have described how you can start interacting with your dog to test and explore which toys and treats he likes, and I said you should play with your dog as if you are five years old, without any inhibitions or cares in the world. You need to be silly and a bit goofy, make lots of stupid noises, and do whatever it takes to get your dog to look at you and wag his tail. Basically I want you to 'be more dog'!

Think back to when you have seen two playful dogs meeting up in the park off lead. They slowly approach each other maintaining eye contact until they are both standing quite still, with maybe a rather stiff wag of the tail. Then, after a few seconds one of them will jump into a little crouch position with his head down slightly, at which point the other

114

dog will tense up, and they will begin to chase each other around. This may be the point where you lose control of your dog. Hopefully, by now you have realised it's not a very good idea for you to allow your dog to think playing with other dogs is the best thing since sliced bread. Not if you want to enjoy stress-free trips to the park anyway.

Just before the dogs run off together, one of the dogs does a little jump into a crouch, which says to the other dog 'You wanna play? OK, chase me!' That is what you are up against when you go to the park. That's what I need you to recreate with your dog now. I'm not suggesting you take your dog to the park and attempt to get him to chase you there, but I do want you to 'be more dog'.

This can be quite hard at first because for some of us it's been a long time since we were children. We might have forgotten how to play and be silly. But you just have to try, and don't be afraid of messing up. You can be really interesting to your dog, but he just doesn't know it yet. Interaction or playing with your dog is like going to the gym and using a muscle that you haven't used for a while. It's really hard at first. It feels awkward and you might feel like quitting, but don't. Once you get past that awkward stage, things get a little easier, and pretty soon you will start lifting heavier weights and feeling fitter and experiencing all the awesome feelings that come with that.

You are reading this because you want your dog not to run away or pull on the lead, or you want him to be more obedient. Well, you first need him to be more interested in you, and we do that by teaching him that actually you are a fun person to be with. If you do nothing else but start playing with your dog regularly as I have described, you will build a great relationship with him, and your whole life with your dog will be much more enjoyable.

You will be a better owner too, one who knows what his dog likes, and eventually you will have much more control on walks because you will have what my good friend David Davies calls the invisible leash. This is where you are connected by more than just a physical lead, and your dog comes back to you and stays near you because he wants to be with you rather than because you restrained him or are shouting at him.

So playing with a toy involves you choosing a toy (or thing) and you getting on the floor and playing with him.

Exercise: Playing with toys

Start at home in your front room or somewhere with low distractions, and you will be less self-conscious.

Take the item that became Kryptonite number five on the list of your dog's favourite items. Before you begin this game, try and have two of the items and make sure they are almost identical, so two socks or hairbrushes or two balls, etc.

Then get your dog's attention (say his name in a cheery voice), and when he looks at you, start talking to him about this wonderful toy, much as you did when you were finding the Kryptonite earlier in the chapter. Keep talking, and you will gradually build his interest and desire to get the toy, but don't give it to him yet. Tease him a little with it if you have to, but remember not to do this if he is normally in any way possessive over a toy as this will just piss him off. Speak in a high-pitched voice, and see what he reacts to. Then when he does something like come towards you, sit in front of you, or even just look at you, show him the toy and see how he reacts.

Does he want it very badly? Is he whining or pawing at you, is he wagging his tail, and does he look happy? Can you make him any more interested by talking to him and telling him how awesome the toy is?

You are basically looking for some kind of reaction from your dog that you wouldn't normally have got. If at this point you normally just throw your toy for your dog, then this time maybe wait a while for him to sit or give you eye contact. It's at that moment you can tell him what a good boy he is and share the toy with him. If he doesn't do anything, then maybe move the toy around, and see if by moving it above his head, you can 'lure' him into a 'sit'. (Basically by just using the toy and your encouraging voice, what can you get him to do for you?) You are not allowed to say 'Sit' yet even if he knows that command.

If you find yourself in a position where you get no reaction at all from your dog, then you need to work a bit harder; maybe get on the floor with him, make the toy move around on the floor, and encourage your dog to chase it. These toys have been ranked in order of how much your dog likes them, so play or interaction time should be quite easy. Your dog may not, however, associate you with the fun of the toy, so keep working hard to get his interest. You are trying to convince the dog that playing a game with you and the toy is more fun than him having the toy to himself.

Of course, he could just be having an off day, so don't stress too much if nothing happens; you can just try again tomorrow. In the meantime, make sure you don't leave the play toys lying around on the floor, and put them away. You could carry one around the house with you, or play a game of pass with your partner; then when the dog shows an interest, you can put the thing away. Do this a few times, and you should soon build some desire for the thing you want to use.

This play or interacting is the start of you connecting with your dog. It's very important for a number of reasons.

By controlling all of the things your dog likes all of a sudden, you instantly raise your status in his eyes, and you become more interesting to him just by association.

By playing and talking you are actually teaching him your language. You will pick up bits of your dog's body language too, but it's more important that he knows your language and what you want from him. So by doing very basic things such as showing him a toy (something he likes) and getting him to do something (eye contact or a 'sit') and then rewarding him, you are showing him what he needs to do to get a reward (the thing he wants).

It's also great fun! For many of the people within my Superhero Dog Owners Inner Circle, the dog audit is the turning point in their relationship with their dogs. This is where they realise their dogs will listen to them and do what they want, even if it's just giving eye contact for one of their favourite toys.

So once you have some focus and reaction, you can continue, and there are two great games you can also play. The first is two toys...

The game of two toys

The basic premise of two toys is you have two toys (or two hairbrushes or plastic bottles or whatever it is that was on the list of things your dog loved). The toys should be almost identical otherwise the dog will prefer one over the other. First get your dog interested in one of the toys; then throw or drop the toy a short distance away. When he goes off to see what you have thrown, take out the second toy and start getting him interested in that. Dogs usually want what someone else has got, so you can make your toy seem more interesting by using your voice and the way you act. Say your dog's name in a nice cheery voice. Move away from him with it slightly and he may follow; then keep talking to your toy, throw it up and catch it, and make stupid noises, 'Whoop whoop!'

The moment your dog drops the first toy, you can drop or throw the one you are holding for him, and then you pick up the first one and start the process again. Try and drop the second toy on the other side of where you dropped the first. If you make yourself the centre of the game with toys being dropped either side of where you are standing, you will be able to retrieve the dropped toys and control the game better.

This is all rather high energy, and dogs really love it. It's very important you don't try and take the toy from the dog, but rather wait for him to drop it. That way he learns when he drops a toy he actually gets another one, so this game is going to teach him that he doesn't need to run off with things, and it's better to share them with you.

You should be talking to your dog and praising him the whole time, especially when he drops the toy and comes towards you for the toy you are holding.

If you are really struggling to get your dog to drop the first toy you threw, then use one of the more desirable items of Kryptonite from the list. You know he likes a number two or three toy more than a five, so use it. See, there is a method in my madness.

The second game is tuggy tugg tugg.

Tuggy tugg tugg

Once again, you shouldn't play this game if your dog is normally possessive over his toys, but most dogs will be fine with it.

You can play tuggy with anything at all that both you and your dog can safely hold, but it's easier if it's a cloth or rope-type material. An old towel or tea towel cut into one- to two-foot long strips with a knot at each end does the job perfectly. I have never met a dog yet who refused to play a game with me because I wasn't using a branded dog toy...

So first get the toy and make it 'come alive', much the same as you did for the other game, only this time you are going to encourage your dog to get hold of it. Don't try and force the toy on him, or he will likely back away from you. You can throw it a short distance or run with it or make it move around the floor and encourage your dog to 'get it'.

You should be telling your dog he is a 'Good boy' every time he looks interested or moves towards the toy and also if he attempts to mouth it.

When he does finally hold the toy, tell him he is a 'Good boy' and have a short game of tuggy. You need to judge this as you play, but don't be too physical at first, and when your dog gets into it, just stop moving the toy. Keep your arm still and wait for him to let go. And wait and wait. You may have to put two hands on the toy (one on either end of the toy with your dog's grip in the middle). Then, and this is the important bit, when he does let go, tell him in a very cheery voice that he's a good boy! And give him his end of the toy straight back again and have another short game of tuggy. Continue this five or six times and then stop. Go and make yourself a brew as a reward and have a sit-down and think about what you did. Your dog can enjoy a biscuit at the same time.

Remember the idea is you are teaching the dog that it's more fun to play with you than it is to keep, run off with, and chew up the toy. So you need to teach him that the game does not end when the pulling and letting go stops, and it will start back up again. Obviously the game has to end sometime, and when it does, you can just tell your dog he is a very good boy and give him some affection. Leaving him wanting more isn't a bad thing.

You should play this game little and often, and always remember to put the toy away when you are finished playing. Don't fall into the trap of telling your dog to 'LEAVE IT' every two seconds, much better to just wait until he lets go. If you really struggle to get him to leave it, exchange a treat for the toy and then resume the game.

And that's tuggy tugg tugg. It's a great physical game, which most dogs really love. Unlike a retrieving game, it keeps your dog near you all the time, and for dogs that really enjoy playing, it can be a great high-energy reward for doing something they like.

Be careful if you are playing this game with puppies – if you are too vigorous, you can easily pull their teeth out. Also, when you are playing tuggy, try and use a forward-and-back motion rather than side to side, as playing tuggy with a side-to-side action can mimic a killing action for a dog.

So this has been a busy old chapter. By now you should have a list of toys your dog likes playing with, his favourite foods, where he likes to be touched and stroked, his five favourite people in the world, and the five most stimulating locations. You also know how to use the Kryptonite to play and interact with your dog.

Here is a checklist once again for your dog audit:

- Find your dog's Kryptonite
- Keep it special
- Start playing with your dog somewhere with low distractions
- Play with your dog little and often
- Enjoy it!

Don't be afraid to screw up, ever!

Final exercise:

You MUST do this exercise because it is very powerful and will save you untold heartache later on. Sometime today I want you to pick one of your dog's less desirable items of Kryptonite, such as his number-five toy or food item. Then I want you to go outside into your garden or yard and try and play the same game with your dog. Use the exact same technique you did indoors and just play with him. As you are playing, watch your dog to see if he acts any differently to when he was indoors. Do this today, and we will come back to this a little later.

Who's a good boy?

You won't hear this on dog training courses or read it anywhere else, but walking and exercising your dog can be a real pain in the arse, can't it? All that pulling on the lead really hurts, and when he ignores you when you let him off lead, it's rather embarrassing too. I used to find it really tiring, and I'm sure my dog didn't enjoy it very much either. Day after day I would come home after a walk sick of the sound of my own voice telling my dog off all the time, 'Come back', 'Get back', 'Leave that', 'Leave him', 'Get down', etc. Well, if you have ever felt like that too, then this chapter shows you how you can change all of that and start enjoying your dog again.

If you look back through this chapter and count up how many times I said talk to your dog in a cheery voice and tell him he's a good boy, you would count five. Basically, every time he does something you want, you need to tell him he is a good boy.

Playing with your dog this way is going to make you both much happier, and owning a dog will be much less stressful. Yes, we have a long way to go with the training, but let's start by enjoying ourselves a bit.

So who is a good boy? Well, tell him and then he will know. Your dog will like being a good boy, and if it's pleasurable enough for him, he will want to do whatever it takes to be a good boy to get the reward from you.

So that is the first stage of the dog audit done. If you have done this correctly and have a list of things your dog loves, then you probably know more about your dog than 80% of the dog owners on the planet.

If you haven't, then go back and do it again. Trust me, just doing this audit and going through the play-with-your-dog process will profoundly change your life. Your dog will look at you differently now: with respect and interest. After all, you control the good things in life, so why wouldn't he be more interested in you?

So what now? Well, you can stay at this stage for a little or a lot longer and just enjoy your dog at home where it's safe. But if you want to enjoy that same kind of playing experience with your dog outside, then we need to take it up a notch and start getting your dog to earn the rewards he so loves. And we do that by attempting a little thing called dog training... you may have heard of it.

Now this isn't the bit where you put the book down because it's too complicated and you think you won't be able to train your dog: far from it! You have been teaching your dog already by teaching him to play with you, so this follows on nicely. In any case, we are going to train with my unique spin, so you and your dog are guaranteed to enjoy it.

Chapter summary

- ◎ Using the toys, treats, and other things your dog likes will give you an easy way to start bonding with him. But don't expect him to start doing backflips or rollovers just because you are holding his favourite toy. How interesting your dog finds you and your relationship with him will improve over time, so keep at it with the games, and treat any increased interest from him as a small success.

- ◎ Don't just shove the treat or toy in your dog's face, or he may back away. Far better to tease your dog and try and make him come towards you. Most dogs will chase things that move, so use the different items of Kryptonite to 'be more dog' and encourage him to move. With some hard work, pretty soon you will have a remote-controlled dog that you can make do all kinds of things using all the resources you discover when you do your dog audit.

◎ This is the moment in the book when you go from learning how to play with and train your dog to actually playing with and training him. You should be looking forward to this because you will thoroughly enjoy finding out what your dog likes. Remember action equals transformation, so get on the floor and play. The more you play and convince your dog that you are an awesome person, the easier it will be to fix the bad behaviours you don't want him to exhibit.

CHAPTER 7

TRAINING MORE THAN ONE DOG

So do these training methods still work if you own more than one dog? Yes, dear reader, rest assured they work if you have three, four, or even more dogs. I have two dogs, many of my clients own two dogs, AND we exercise the dogs daily in groups of up to 10 dogs.

However, there is a slight caveat to that. If you really want to improve the relationship you have with each of your dogs, then you will have to spend more time alone with each dog individually than you do now.

Remember your dog is going to be most influenced by whoever or whatever he spends the most time with and consequently gets the most fun, stimulation, and excitement from. And if you have two or more dogs, then their main stimulation is probably going to come from each other.

So unless you have lots of time to devote to playing and training, then your dogs are going to spend more time with each other than they are with you.

There are two ways to look at this, of course. One is that the dogs will bond really well because they play, eat, and sleep together and the other is that as they bond so well because they play, eat, and sleep together, you, the owner, become less relevant to them. Let me explain that in a bit more detail.

We have already discussed how the easiest way to have a dog that listens to you is to be the most interesting thing in his life. So the ideal is to be the one person that your dog looks to for all his affection, fun, entertainment, food, and exercise. If you do this, then you will have an amazing bond together. Well, you don't need to be a dog psychologist to see that this becomes much harder to achieve when you throw another dog into the mix.

One dog at a time

I own two dogs, and I can tell you from experience that it's twice as hard (and more) to train two dogs than just one. I'm not down on people owning two or more dogs, but it's a fact that the more dogs you add to your family, the less time you will be able to spend with each individual dog. The likelihood that some of your dogs will develop behaviour problems may then increase.

There are a couple of ways this usually happens. The most common is that someone owns a dog that is generally pretty well behaved and they decide at some point that they would like another dog. The second 'new' dog receives some basic training, but because of work and general life commitments he ends up spending the majority of his time with the first dog.

The first dog is usually fine with this, hopefully he is anyway, and the first dog will be older and usually the calmer of the two. The second or new dog spends so much time with the first dog that he sees being with another dog as the norm, in just the same way as the first dog was happy to be on his own.

In cases where the dogs do everything together, the second dog will end up seeing the first dog as his keeper and not you, the owner. In time he may become very dependent on being with another dog.

The first dog may be man's (or the owner's) best friend, but the second dog becomes a dog's best friend. The age and temperament of the first/older dog will have a big influence on how the younger dog turns out. If you already have a dog-reactive dog that is difficult to control, then unless you do a lot of training, it's highly likely you will end up with two out-of-control dogs that are difficult to manage.

Another example would be the owner who decides to take two puppies from a litter instead of just one. I know what you are thinking. What would be cuter and more exciting than getting a puppy, eh? What about getting two! Sadly, two sibling puppies rarely work out trouble-free. I have worked with clients who have done this, and the common theme every time is a lack of control over the dogs. That's not to say it's impossible to have two well-behaved dogs from the same litter, but getting two dogs like this sets it up from the outset to be much more difficult for you.

Think about it; the puppies come to you already incredibly well bonded as they have been together with their mother every day since they were born. By the time puppies are seven or eight weeks old, which is the time they would leave and join a new home, they have done all the dog-to-dog socialisation they need to do; they have learned how to play, and how to bite, all under the careful supervision of the mother.

Then a new stage of a puppy's life begins, and he learns how to bond and play with his new human family. During the crucial first four months, he is gradually and carefully exposed to things like cars, buses, carrier bags, fireworks, lollipop men, and everything else we want to get the puppy used to, so he grows into a confident, happy dog.

For a puppy that's raised on his own, other dogs will hopefully just be something that he treats the same way as he does birds he encounters on a walk or the bin lorry, i.e. something he sees on a regular basis but is nothing to get particularly excited about.

This is much harder to achieve when the main thing a puppy spends its time with is another puppy. We already know that dogs are playful; well, puppies are even more so. I can tell you from experience it can be hard enough to get one puppy to listen to you, so trust me; training two will be more than twice as hard.

Remember I'm coming at this from the sole objective of wanting to have an easy and happy life with my dog. So if you own more than one dog, then complete the dog audit for each dog you own and then prioritise spending time with each dog individually, giving more time to the dog that needs the most work. You will know which of your dogs doesn't listen to you as much, pulls on the lead more, or is more reactive to other dogs you meet, so prioritise and try and fix the biggest problem first.

There really is no silver bullet with this. I have helped many clients (both online and in person) who owned two or more dogs, and the ones who were most successful spent more time with each of their dogs individually, building up a better bond and finding out what each dog liked, and then used that information to influence their dogs and better control them.

To me it makes way more sense to spend 10 minutes with each of my dogs individually, playing a game or practising a few tricks, than struggling to play with both my dogs at the same time and not really giving either the attention they want. I should also add that all of the owners reported that they really enjoyed this extra time they put into their dogs' training. Think of it as a daddy (or a mammy) date night that you get to enjoy with each of your dogs whenever you like.

So if you have more than one dog, then you know what to do, and if you have one dog and are thinking of getting another, remember that you can provide all of the fun, stimulation, and excitement your dog will ever need and he doesn't need another dog in his life to be happy.

Chapter summary

- The key with dog training is consistency. The more time you spend regularly training your dog to enjoy doing things with you, the easier he will be to control. This is also true if you own more than one dog. You can teach your pack to ignore other dogs and do exactly what you want, but you may find the easiest way to do this is with each dog individually first.

- This is exactly what I do when we introduce another dog to our group adventures. After an assessment, I will work, walk, and play with that dog on his own for a few weeks, until I have built up enough drive for a toy and taught him a few games to enjoy with it. I am basically teaching the dog that I am a really fun person to be with, so when he starts coming out with our pack, then his focus is more on me than the other dogs. It can be done.

◎ There will be people you know who own two dogs who will no doubt tell you how great it is to own two dogs. That their dogs get on fabulously well together and they would have 10 dogs if they could… Well, now you know a little better, so when you catch anyone saying that, just smile and nod and continue on your merry way with your one dog that thinks the sun shines out of your arse.

CHAPTER 8
WHERE AND WHAT SHOULD YOU TEACH YOUR DOG?

Imagine you are the boss of a construction company and you are submitting a bid to a chain of hotels to build their next one. There is a lot riding on this project, and you have to get the tender correct in order to save your company's immediate future and the jobs of thousands of employees. Bid too little and your company and all its employees are jobless. Bid too much and you may win, but you won't make much profit and so won't secure your company's future. Wow, that's a lot of pressure.

Now imagine the tender fairy comes along and whispers into your ear the exact amount of money you need to bid to secure the deal, save the jobs, and also make a nice wedge too.

You would be pretty silly not to use that information, wouldn't you?

Well, you now know exactly what your dog likes, so we are going to use that info to get him to do stuff for us. How cool is that!

Before we dive into the how, let's briefly look at where and what you should teach your dog.

Where should you train your dog?

Let's talk about where you should train your dog first because this is where most dog owners make life incredibly and unnecessarily hard for themselves. I want you to enjoy an easy life with your dog, so if you follow what I tell you now, you will save yourself untold stress, anger, and frustration in the coming weeks and possibly for the rest of your life.

You need to give some thought to where you play with, exercise, and train your dog from now on. You can't just expect that once you have made a connection and your dog is enjoying playing two toys with you in your living room that he is going to want to do that in the park. There will be way too many distractions there, and he will associate that place with chasing birds or playing with other dogs or whatever it was that he has always done there. Don't think that he won't, because he will. There's no getting round this, I'm afraid, and you will set yourself up for failure if you return to all the old haunts where your dog used to act up and misbehave.

This is why in the previous chapter I got you to identify and write down the top five places where your dog was most stimulated. Now look at that list again, and don't go to any of those places on the list. If you must, then don't expect him to take any notice of you when you get there, if he didn't take any notice of you before you started reading this book. Old habits die hard for dogs too.

As a basic rule of thumb, the more stimulating the environment, the harder it is to get and keep your dog's attention on you. So I would recommend you start the playing and training with the following exercises at home in your living room, then move on to the kitchen. When you have nailed an exercise there, then take it out into your garden or yard, and only then should you think about going further afield to a quiet area of your park.

Why so slow? Because it's easier that way, silly, and Dom is all about making things easy! Of course you may love the stress of chasing your dog around the park or shouting at him to get his attention on you, and if that sounds like you, then crack on, my friend.

However, if you want some peace in your life, just do as I say and you can thank me later.

Remember back to how your dog learns things. He learns by doing something, and if he enjoys it, he will want to do it again. Well, if your dog has learned that when he goes to the park he gets to play with other dogs or chase birds, and he has had an opportunity to practise that behaviour over time, then it is going to be a very deeply embedded behaviour.

You can't unlearn what you have learned. It's done already, and your dog isn't just going to forget that he loves playing with other dogs. We can only teach him something different to do instead. That is what we will do now, but we are going to remove the thing that is currently too distracting for him and not go to the park.

Imagine you are treating a drug addict who is fresh out of rehab. As part of the rehabilitation you would probably recommend that he doesn't hang around drug dealers for a while, wouldn't you? The temptation would just be too great until he had built up some willpower and developed some coping strategies to help him. Well, by avoiding the park or the beach or wherever it is that your dog is attracted to that bird or dog or desirable thing that makes him naughty, we are going to remove it from the equation.

And walks are way overrated anyway. You can have loads of fun with your dog at home or in your garden. Unless your dog is a puppy that must be out every day socialising and getting used to experiencing all of the different things you want him to be OK with when he is older, then your dog doesn't need to go to the park every day. This isn't the end of you being able to take your dog to the park, but maybe just put a pin in the walks that cause the most stress for now.

The more reclusive a person you are, the easier you will find this. If you enjoy the social side of walking your dog, but you know that your dog plays like a loon with a friend's dog in the park every day, then you have a difficult decision to make. It will be easier if you explain to your friend that you are doing some new training programme and you think you'll have more success if you exercise your dog alone for a few weeks. Give them a copy of the book if they don't believe you. Of course, it's always your choice, but certainly you will progress a lot quicker if you completely avoid the park for a month or so.

But don't worry; because you are going to start enjoying your own dog a lot more when you take him out. Playtime will involve you from now on and not another dog or pigeon.

Warning

Be very wary of joining dog socialisation walks run by wannabe dog whisperers who think throwing a load of dogs together to 'socialise' is a good idea. These walks are often run by very well-meaning dog lovers, but they don't understand the consequences of letting dogs play together for a couple of hours once a week. You know the repercussions for the dog owners when they exercise them for the rest of the week.

The people who do best on my online programme are the ones that start slowly and enjoy training and playing with their dogs *at home*. They practise and lock down a new trick or game in the sitting room, and then they make sure their dog really enjoys doing it in the kitchen and the garden BEFORE moving on to the park. This allows you gradually to build up a new pattern of behaviour for your dog.

So if you want an easy life now, you know where to train your dog. But, what exactly should you teach him?

What to teach your dog

When you think of dog training, you may have visions of a sergeant-major-type character who shows you how to march around a field anticlockwise with your dog marking out a perfect square (because that's normal, isn't it?). And you must always set off on the left foot first (like the dog gives a shit which foot you set off on). And if he strays slightly forward, you must say HEEL DOG and pull him towards you (because that will make him want to do it, won't it?)

Of course not all dog-training classes are like that, but they do exist. I know some amazing dog trainers who run fantastic classes where you learn new things together that help you improve the relationship between you and your dog. But some of them teach the most pointless exercises that do nothing to help an owner get their dog more interested in them and have little value to anyone who lives in the real world.

I would also avoid any training class where the dogs or puppies are encouraged to have 10 minutes' 'free play'. It's likely that this free play will be the one thing your dog will enjoy the most AND remember from the class, and so will be the one thing he wants to do again when he sees another dog.

The best advice would be to go along to a class BEFORE you get your puppy or dog and see exactly what is taught. You need to question whether the class will help you teach your dog that you're the most interesting thing in his world and make him easier to walk and live with.

So I personally like to teach my dogs stuff to do that is going to keep them close to me and make them want to be with me. And we are going to start with your dog's name.

What does your dog's name mean to him?

"It ain't what they call you; it's what you answer to."
—*W.C. Fields*

I think the most important thing you will ever teach your dog is his name and that saying his name means he should either look at you or come to you. Some trainers will say that a 'stop' command or a 'leave it' is more important, but I think it will help you most if you teach your dog to enjoy being with you all of the time. We are going to start that by making your dog think that something awesome is going to come from you whenever he hears his name.

I like my dog to associate hearing his name with a recall, because whether you like it or not, your dog's name is the thing you usually say when you want them to come.

That's why we started the eye contact exercise in chapter 1. Rewarding your dog with a smile, a 'good boy' or a pat on the head (or even all three) every time he gives you eye contact is going to build up a great association in his mind of why he should look at you when he hears his name. You should continue to reward eye contact as often as you can to build on this. Turn every meal or treat time into an opportunity to further practise focusing on eye contact.

Exercise: 'Watch me'

Next time you go to give your dog a treat, say his name and wait for him to give you eye contact before you give it to him. This may take a while at first because he may be focused on the treat, so be patient. As soon as his eyes hit yours, say, 'Good boy'. When he is doing it regularly, you can start to say 'Watch me' or 'Watch' or whatever you prefer. You can practise this further at meal times and ask your dog to 'Watch me' before you feed him. You could be extra smart and split the meal into five portions and practise a 'Watch me' before you feed him each bowl. This is the little-and-often way of training your dog, and it's one I prefer. Far better to make playing and interacting with your dog and training and challenging him part of your everyday routine than embarking on some intensive and serious training session where you put too much pressure on yourself to succeed. It's like the benefits of eating healthily all year round, rather than losing 10 pounds in a two-week crash diet where you inevitably end up back where you started.

Once you are having regular success with the 'Watch me' exercise, you should develop it into a 'catch-up' game.

The catch-up game

This game can be played with food or toys as well as affection, and it puts the emphasis on your dog being rewarded for coming to you. This enables you to practise a recall many times every day, in your home and garden.

By now your dog should be responding well when he hears his name called by you. Dogs love attention, and if the consequence of him giving you his attention is rewarded regularly, then he will do it more often. Not only that, he will want to do it and should start following you more because he associates being with you as enjoyable.

You should use low-value treats for this exercise such as a number four or five from the list you made earlier in your dog audit. Similarly use a low-value toy, preferably two that are identical. Of course, if you have been practising or if your dog is responding well to the sound of your voice, then don't use any toys at all; just use affection and praise.

Let's assume you have a bowl of your dog's mixer to hand. Take a small handful and show your dog one of the pieces, then throw the treat a metre or two away, but so your dog sees it being thrown. Your dog should go and retrieve the treat from the floor. Then just as he eats it, call his name in your happy dog voice, and as he comes towards you, wave another treat at him. As he gets near to you, throw that treat to the side of you that's furthest away from the direction he is coming from. Again, not too far away, you want him to get the reward. As soon as he collects that treat or toy, you should call his name again. As he gets quicker, you can increase the distance you throw the treat. Also, as he is retrieving the treat, you can walk in the opposite direction, so he has a bit further to come to you.

When your dog has the idea, you can start mixing it up a bit. Every third or fourth go, don't throw a treat, and instead, when he gets to you praise him, stroke his ears and tell him what a brilliant dog he is. Then start the game again, and this time on the third go, when he is retrieving the thrown treat, say his name, and when he comes towards you, have three treats ready in your hand to reward him with. Dogs are eternal chancers, and mixing up the rewards like this will keep him guessing as to what he is going to get next.

This game can then be taken into the garden, and it's a good game to play in the park with your dog on a long lead if you wish. Remember, you may need to use a higher-value item of Kryptonite when you are exercising somewhere with more distractions.

The 'Watch me' and 'catch-up' games are games you can and should play whenever you feed or play with your dog.

You can't ban the fun, so be the fun instead

From 1920 to 1933, prohibition was in effect throughout the United States of America. However, the government struggled to enforce the legislation, which banned the manufacture, transportation, and sale of intoxicating liquor. This was just as well because a large portion of the population across all classes of society enjoyed a drink. Actually drinking alcohol wasn't illegal, so drink it they continued to do. They sometimes made do with moonshine or home-made bathtub gin, or more usually enjoyed the whisky and rum that flowed in illegal speakeasies right across the country. The point is you can't just ban something that people enjoy and expect them not to find another way to get what they want.

And so it is with your dog. You have identified all the places and triggers that cause your dog to be badly behaved, and hopefully I have convinced you by now that if you want to improve your dog's behaviour, then you need to start doing something different. We already know that play, interaction, and challenge are key daily needs that require fulfilling for our dogs, so if we are going to stop them from having fun one way, we need to replace that with another kind of fun. And that is having fun with us.

Many training clients begin the process of bonding and playing with and training their dog, but then too quickly they rush off to the park to see if their dog's behaviour is any better. My advice to you is **not to do that** as inevitably your dog will quickly revert back to the bad behaviour he used to exhibit in that place. To see a lasting change in your dog, you need to completely avoid where he is naughty for around a month or so; six weeks would be even better.

If you had a sharp intake of breath at my suggestion that you don't go to the park for six weeks, then hear me out. This is going to be easier than you think, and there are three good reasons why you should follow my plan.

1) It works. Yes, it really does. If you were having a training consultation with me in person, the first thing I would do would be to identify the problem and advise you to avoid it completely where possible. Then we would begin teaching your dog something new to do instead.

2) Avoiding the thing your dog doesn't like makes it much easier for you to teach him something new. If he's distracted, then you won't have his attention, and without his attention you might as well not bother. Then you will get frustrated at your dog and end up feeling like a failure. To avoid this and make it as easy as possible for your dog to associate being with **you** with having fun, you should remove anything else he may find interesting. This doesn't completely solve the problem, but it makes it a lot more likely you will succeed. Think of it like starting a diet. The chances of you snacking on some strawberries when you feel a little peckish rather than p-p-picking up a Penguin will be much greater if you have stocked up on some ripe and tasty fruits and thrown away all of the biscuits before you start.

3) Your life will be better. Yes, that is a lofty claim for a dog walker from Sunderland to make, but it's true. By following this plan you will remove lots of stress from your life almost overnight.

Think of it like trying to lose weight, which is something that I struggle with from time to time. You start by seeing what weight you are and decide on a target weight. Then you might join a gym, start running, or follow a training plan, which will help you gradually move towards your target weight. But the training is just part of the equation because if you continue to sneak a chocolate bar or a slice of pizza every day, you sabotage your chances of getting to your target weight. You may still lose some, but you don't ever end up getting the result you wanted at the start.

This does require a small shift in mindset from you. Start thinking of your dog as someone that needs safety, exercise, interaction, and challenge in his life rather than a walk to the park. There is no need for you to continue to take your dog for a trip to the park if all he does is misbehave and stress you out. So, I know you don't need it, but you have my permission not to take your dog to the park for the next six weeks. In fact, I heartily recommend it.

So what will you do instead?

Well, that's what we will find out in the next chapter.

Chapter summary

◎ It's vital to ensure that your dog's learning environment is as distraction-free as possible. I remember when I was in a science class at school and there were a couple of pigeons screwing on the roof opposite; I couldn't concentrate for love nor money. Well, your dog will be as easily distracted as I was by anything that moves, not to mention any smells, which obviously you can't see. So play with him and train him somewhere quiet, or better still, stay at home.

◎ Think about your dog's name and more importantly what he thinks of when he hears his name. If he associates his name with a pleasant experience, then he will come to you and listen to you quickly, which will make controlling him much easier. Get in the habit of rewarding eye contact often, and especially reward him when he offers you eye contact of his own accord. If your dog regularly checks in with you, it will make for stress-free walks.

◎ When it comes to what you actually train your dog to do, the list is varied and almost endless. Not everything I teach in the book will work with every dog, but there are games, tricks, and exercises to suit any dog, so try everything at least once. I like to play games that keep my dogs close by me and you should too, because that way your walks will be safer and eventually you will be able to exercise your dog anywhere off lead. This is the nirvana for all dog owners.

CHAPTER 9
HOW TO TEACH YOUR DOG ANYTHING

"Tell me and I forget, teach me and I may remember, involve me and I learn."
— Benjamin Franklin

This is Aster, one of my regular adventure and boarding clients. Isn't she pretty?

Aster is going to help you remember how to teach your dog anything using the luring method.

But first we need to lose the 'e' from her name so we are left with ASTR, which stands for:

A – Attention

S – Show

T – Tell

R – Reward

Luring is all about showing your dog what you want them to do. Think of it as using something like a ball or food to guide your dog into whatever position you want him in. Let's use teaching a 'sit' as an example, so I can explain how using ASTR works.

The five tricks every dog should know

'Sit'

First make sure your dog has seen the toy or treat by putting it in front of his face (or nose for food). This is you getting your dog's ATTENTION.

Slowly move your hand holding the treat from his nose to just above his head. Then wait for him to put his bum on the floor. If he doesn't, just take it back to his nose again, and move it even more slowly above his head. Maybe change the angle this time, so you are going more above his head then back towards his neck (slowly) or above his head towards you. Take your time with this and be patient. Your dog doesn't know what you want him to do, but he will do very soon, and once he's got it, he will easily do it all. This is you SHOWING your dog what you want him to do.

Once your dog has done it a few times, you can TELL him the command. So once he starts sitting regularly, you should then say 'Sit'. Remember your dog doesn't speak English, and it's much easier to pair the command to the action than it is to repeat 'Sit' 17 times while you wait for your dog to sit.

As soon as your dog's bum hits the floor, you say 'Good boy' and give him his REWARD (a game of tug or a little piece of kibble). Repeat this and once your dog has done it four or five times and has the idea, you can start to add the 'Sit' as his bum hits the floor. That's your 'Tell', so you tell him what you want. Repeat another four or five times until he is sitting as you say 'Sit'.

Once your dog has the hang of it, try to lure him into position using just your hand. Place the Kryptonite on a bench or in your pocket. Then when he sits, get the Kryptonite out, make a huge fuss, and have a nice game or a little piece of food.

You should repeat this until you think your dog is doing the action when you say the command almost every time; then put the toys and treats to one side and have a little break.

In the break you should put the kettle on and tell your dog how bloody clever you think he is, give him some affection, and check out his five favourite places to be stroked again to see if any of them have changed. I want you to go overboard with the affection and the praise. Your dog will enjoy it, and he will associate the whole training session with having a good time with you. Using lots of praise and affection will mean you are not completely dependent on the toys and treats to keep your dog's focus on you. You will enjoy it too.

So there you go; that's how to teach a 'sit' using luring, and you have ASTR to help you remember. It's not hard at all, is it?

No, Dom, it isn't.

But it's only easy because you did the dog audit and you know what your dog likes.

Don't forget you need to have your dog's attention first, so you should always play with him a little before you start. Think of this as a warm-up.

Training tips:

Be careful you don't use too high a value item of Kryptonite when you begin your training indoors. There are a couple of reasons for this.

Using a treat that is too tasty or a toy that is too stimulating is going to have your dog jumping at you to get at it. You want to use something that he wants, but that he won't go mental for, so use a number four or five item of Kryptonite from your list.

The other reason is you will need to use the higher-value items when you take the training outside and there are more distractions around. Also, it just makes more sense to train this way.

If you were starting a new job, and you got a bonus and a new car as soon as you walked in the door, then you may struggle to get motivated as every day after that is not as good as your first. So, let's think long term and make our dogs work a little even for a low-value treat. Of course, you are going to use your voice and affection to make even the low-value Kryptonite feel rewarding for your dog.

So where do we go now? Well, if you really want to progress with your training, you should do two things.

1) Start teaching another trick. I would recommend a 'down' then 'spin' followed by 'catch it' and then 'through the legs'. I have instructions for you to follow so you can teach each new trick using the same luring technique and ASTR just as you did with the 'sit'.

2) But just as important as starting something new is to lock down the trick you have just taught. So start practising your 'sit' in the kitchen and other rooms in the house, BEFORE you do the same thing in the garden, street, and eventually the park. Don't expect your dog to sit automatically straightaway in another room on command, but you should be able to teach him the same trick in the kitchen that you did elsewhere.

Make it easy for yourself and have your Kryptonite to hand. You probably won't need to do as much luring as you did in the sitting room, or if you do, you will more quickly be able to start luring with just your hand, but be prepared to use some toys or treats to get him going. One thing you absolutely must do is talk to your dog; say his name, and use praise and affection before, during, and after whenever you practise anything. Then he will have fun and enjoy it, and he will want to do it again.

The second point is very important, as this whole trick section is the start of us building a routine of things to do with our dog on a daily basis wherever we go. We are going to have a whole routine of things that we do with our dog that he loves, but we have to start learning where it's easiest to learn, indoors, then gradually move out and up the Kryptonite as and when we need it, depending on the distractions. This takes a bit of time, and you can't just jump from the living room to the park, so be patient and build up steadily the way I describe. Slowly introduce distractions, and most importantly make everything fun for the dog. Your dog doesn't really want a rabbit or a dog or an empty pizza box; that's just something he has learned to go after because it excites him. Your dog wants some fun and entertainment in his life, so that's what you have to be!

Teaching other tricks:

'Down'

You can lure your dog to a 'down' from a 'sit' or a 'stand'. I will describe it from a 'sit' as that's the exercise we have just done, but feel free to go from a 'stand' or whatever is easier for you.

So think ASTR, and first get your Kryptonite and get your dog's attention.

From a 'sit' position, move your hand from your dog's face area (to make sure he has seen the toy or smelt the food) and slowly move your hand down towards the floor in front of him. You can encourage him to get it or follow it down to the floor. But don't say 'Down' yet, remember. We are at the 'SHOW' part where we show him what we want him to do.

You may have more success moving the toy slowly down between your dog's front paws, and he should slowly slide down into the 'down' position. Again, this isn't a race, so take your time with it.

Dogs are a bit like humans in that some are cleverer and quicker than others, and from experience I can tell you that my Cocker Spaniel, Sid, learned to do a 'sit', 'down', 'spin', and 'rollover' in the time it took me to get some eye contact from Barry. Remember this isn't a competition, and you should challenge and push your dog, but go at a pace that suits him and always make sure it's fun for him. On that subject, with all these exercises and tricks, you should be rewarding your dog for **trying**, so if he even attempts a 'down' and slides down just a little, you should tell him he's a good boy.

Encouragement is the key here. We want him to enjoy it and want to do it again, so make it pleasurable. If you feel yourself getting frustrated with your dog, have time out, remind yourself it's not the dog's fault, and have another go later on.

Training tip:

Some dogs just aren't that keen on a 'down', so don't stress if your dog doesn't fancy it, or maybe try on a different floor surface. If your dog keeps moving backwards, you could try the exercise with your dog's back end facing a wall or your couch. Then as you go from a 'sit' to a 'down', he can't back away from you. This sometimes helps them into a 'down' position. Then as soon as your dog gets near a 'down' position, you can tell him he is a 'Good boy' and give him some affection or a little piece of food. Repeat this, keeping it light and fun. Start getting into a rhythm of practising something five or six times and then having a little break. When your dog is going into a 'down' regularly, you can start to add the 'TELL' ('Down') command as his chest hits the floor. Again, repeat five or six times.

There is a slightly quicker and more direct way to teach this to dogs that are very toy or food motivated. Get down on your haunches with your dog, and make the toy or food 'come alive' to get his attention, and then move your hand from side to side across your dog's face so your dog is following your hand very closely and looks like he is watching a tennis match. Then quite quickly move your hand up just above your dog's head and then quickly down to the floor. If your dog loves the toy or treat you have, he may well jump into a 'down' position, at which point you can reward him with a 'Good boy' and his treat. As before, you should reward for just trying, so if he only goes halfway down, give him a reward a few times, and then gradually wait a little longer until he goes further down before you reward him.

'Spin'

I love 'spin', and I get my dogs to do it all the time when we are out and about. This trick looks great and dogs seem to love it too. Again think ASTR.

Attention – Show your dog the toy or treat. This trick is easier if your dog is standing up, and if he is a dog who likes to move away from you, then you should use a training lead to prevent him doing so.

Show – Show your dog what you want him to do. Hold the reward in front of his face. Imagine your dog is wearing a large top hat and slowly trace a circle around the outer brim of the hat. Your dog should follow your hand and circle round and return to something like the start position.

Tell – Say 'Spin' once he has the idea, and you can lure him fully round quite easily.

Reward – This exercise usually takes a little while, and you should definitely be rewarding your dog for doing a quarter turn and then a half and eventually a full turn.

Take your time with this. A full 'spin' may take a few days or even a week to perfect, but there's no rush to get it done quickly. Once your dog is following the treat and spinning more easily, you should just use the hand movement to trace the circle, and then reward the dog afterwards. Then in time you can fade out the hand movement – you still say 'Spin', but the hand movement is less defined. But this can take many weeks. Don't blame the dog if he doesn't do it straightaway, and give him lots of praise when he starts to turn round. This will make him feel good.

Once you have locked down the 'spin', why not teach him a 'twist'? That's just spinning the opposite way round. So start the whole exercise again, and be prepared for it to take just as long as the 'spin' did.

Training tip:

It's much easier to teach a 'spin' from a standing position. However, if your dog keeps sitting down (which he might well do if that's what you have just taught him), move backwards slightly and tempt him towards you with the treat, then as he stands up and moves, you can start to trace the circle around his head. He will already be moving forward by then, and it's easier to get him to continue the movement but go around than it is to get him to start a 'spin' from a sitting position.

'Catch it'

Some dogs are really great at this game and others not so much. However, if they like food, which most dogs do, then you can easily teach this trick. Dogs that live with young children tend to be pretty good, as they will have had lots of practice catching bits of toast that the toddler has dropped from the high chair.

You should use a fairly large treat for this game – well, compared to the size of your dog, I mean. Don't go throwing Scotch eggs at your Chihuahua.

Position your dog so he is sitting directly in front of you, and show him the treat. Then raise your hand up in front of you so he follows the treat. Repeat a couple of times. Then take half a step back and raise your hand again, and this time gently throw the treat towards your dog. If your dog has never done this before, then take your time. You want the throwing action to be quite slow and exaggerated at first (imagine you are throwing a ball of wool to your grandmother) because you actually want him to catch it. So aim for his mouth if possible.

The pay-off for this trick is pretty instant for your dog, so once he has caught a few treats he should have the idea. Be sure to tell him he is a good boy once he has caught it too.

'Through the legs'

This is another really easy trick, and I like it because it is a fun way to encourage your dog to come back to you.

You can use a toy or a treat, which you should show your dog to get his attention. Then take a step back if you need to get your dog moving forwards and following the reward, and lure him towards you. Place your legs fairly wide apart but so you are comfortable, no full or half splits please… Then drop the toy or treat just between your legs and reward your dog with lots of praise when he picks it up. Repeat this a few times, gradually dropping the toy further behind your legs so your dog has to gradually move further underneath you to get it. Then when he is moving through, you can say 'Under' or 'In there' or whatever you want your TELL command to be.

Training tip:

Always drop the toy through your legs at first, and don't go around the side of your body and drop it behind, or your dog will just follow your hand around your body. Also, don't throw the toy or treat too far between your legs and behind you either. Your dog will probably just run around you to get the toy.

After a few days practising, you should be able to direct your dog between your legs using the command and the action of pretending you are throwing the toy between your legs. Then once your dog runs through, he will look for the toy on the floor, which you will then throw to him and give him lots of praise and affection.

So that's five tricks to start you off. I have picked these because they are fairly easy to teach and I do them myself every day with my own and my clients' dogs.

All of the tricks require your dog to be fairly close to you, so when you practise them you are giving your dog a reason to be near you wherever you are.

Training tricks like these are the next logical step after you have completed the dog audit. So you have found out what your dog likes, the Kryptonite, and you have played with him with the Kryptonite, so he starts to associate you with the

Kryptonite. Teaching and practising these tricks makes your dog earn the rewards instead of just getting them for nothing. If you make this process fun, and you should do, then your dog will start to see you as his superhero, and you will eventually have your very own working pet dog.

Let's address the final exercise at the end of chapter 6, where I wanted you to try playing and interacting with your dog outside and observe if your dog acted any differently. So was he any different in the garden or yard than he was in the house? I'm guessing yes and that he was more distracted outside, because everything is different outside. Our senses are bombarded by stimuli and so are our dogs' senses.

We will go into your dog's nose a little later (not literally), but outside there is more air movement and, especially if you live in the UK, more moisture. Well, scent is moisture, and your dog's nose is going to pick up many more scents than yours. These smells will be interesting to him, and he will want to explore them. This is why you need to spend a lot of time playing indoors and building up a drive that counteracts his desire to want to go and explore every smell that isn't you and your toy.

So the point of the exercise was to highlight how much more easily distracted your dog becomes when he is outside. And if he was more easily distracted, then just think how much more difficult it will be in the park, woods or at the beach, where the sights and smells he encounters will be even more varied and stimulating.

Chapter summary

◎ Use ASTR to help you whenever you teach your dog anything new. If he looks at you blankly, he is not being awkward; he either doesn't know what you want him to do, the reward you are using isn't rewarding enough, or it's too complicated for him. Either way 'it's not the dogs fault', so take it back a few steps or break down the exercise and make it easier for him.

◎ Don't make the mistake of thinking that tricks are just something that dog trainers do. You are your dog's best friend, owner, AND teacher now. Teaching him something new will eventually make it easier for you to distract him from the thing you don't want him to do. Tricks are great fun, and you will surprise yourself by how clever you and your dog really are once you start practising them.

◎ Think back to when you first got your puppy. You were really keen to teach him something new and felt so accomplished when you taught him a 'sit' or 'down'. But did your dog stop learning, or did you stop teaching? Well, you can get that same feeling back every day by practising some new tricks now, and the five I describe above are easy to teach, but challenging enough to make it interesting.

CHAPTER 10
LAZY DOG GAMES

*"What does a dog do on his day off? He can't lie around –
that's his job."*
– George Carlin

I hope by now you can see the benefits of having a dog that thinks you are his superhero. Involving yourself with how he gets rid of his energy by playing games that give him the opportunity to show off his stamina and strength is a great way to play and bond with him. But not all the games we play with our dogs need to be so physical.

There will be occasions in your dog's life when for one reason or another he can't run around, for example, if he cuts a paw, has an operation that requires rest, or indeed just gets a little older and slower.

The following two activities require very little actual movement from your dog (or you), but don't feel like you have to wait until your dog gets an injury before you play these games. You should make them part of your daily routine as they will test and tire your dog mentally, as well as teaching him some self-control.

Teaching a 'leave it'

If you completed the tuggy tugg tugg exercises earlier, then you will see some similarities with this game in how and when we reward the dog.

I suggest using food for this game, and you should start with something that your dog likes eating but is fairly low value for him. So use a number four or five food Kryptonite from your dog audit. If your dog is very food motivated, then you should use a very small piece of food. As always if your dog is very possessive, then maybe avoid this game altogether unless you can get one-to-one help with a dog trainer who can guide you through this safely. Most dogs are fine to be taught to leave it though.

This is also one of the first exercises I teach a puppy, but dogs of any age can and should be taught a 'leave it'.

We will be using ASTR again to help us learn this exercise, so the running order will be…

Attention – Show your dog the treat, and then close your hand around it.

Show – You are going to wait for him to leave it.

Tell – Say 'Leave it'.

Reward – Say 'Good boy' and give him the treat.

And here's a more detailed version:

Stage one:

Start the exercise sitting on a chair with your dog sitting on the floor beside you or in front of you.

Show your dog the small piece of kibble or food. Let him smell it so he knows you have it. Then close your hand into a fist with the treat inside so he can't see it. He will probably move his nose forward to see where the food has gone. If he doesn't, you can move your closed hand under your dog's nose again, so he can smell the treat inside your hand. You want him to be interested in getting the treat but not pawing madly at you.

Most dogs will now be licking your hand and trying to get to the treat. Do not say anything except maybe 'NO' if your dog is too rough, but just wait with your palm closed. And wait. Your dog should be very curious by now and trying to figure out what he has to do to get the food. Sometime in the next minute after trying a few different things, your dog will move his head slightly away from your hand. The very second that he does this, say 'Good boy', open up your hand and say 'Take it', and give him the food.

At first, your dog may not understand why he has been given the food, but if you repeat this a couple more times, the penny will drop and your dog will get the idea that when he moves his head away from the food (association), he actually gets the food (consequence). Repeat five or six times, and then have a little break and a cuppa. Your dog will also benefit from some time to process what he's learned, before you have another go.

When you get to the point where your dog is moving away from your hand more often than he isn't, you should start adding in the 'Leave it' command. You don't need to shout or growl at him at him through gritted teeth though. The game is called 'Leave it' not 'Fucking leave it!', so just say it in your normal voice. In time, he will match the command with the action and will move away when you tell him, but at first you will be saying 'Leave it' as he moves his head away so you are following his movement.

After five minutes or so (may be quicker or longer depending on the dog and how much time you spend practising), you should be in a position where you can show your dog a piece of food, and then close your hand around it and say 'Leave it', and your dog will leave it. He will give you eye contact, at which point you say 'Good boy', and open your hand and then (and only then), when you say 'Take it', can your dog have the treat.

Once your dog gets the idea and is moving away from the treat 80% of the time, you can take the exercise to the next step and wait for him to move his eyes from your hand and look at you before you say 'Good boy'; then you can open your hand and tell him to 'Take it'.

Getting eye contact like this is important. We eventually want your dog to leave anything you tell him to, like dropped food he may come across in the park. The easiest way to get him to ignore something is to get him to look at you instead. If you can get him into the habit of looking at you when you say 'Leave it', this means he will look away from the thing you want him to leave alone. At which point you can tell him he is a good boy, recall him, and reward him with something else that you have on you.

The routine then becomes leave it, eye contact, good boy, take it, reward.

You should repeat the exercise a couple of times a day over the next day or two. When you know your dog has got it and understands that the best and only way he is going to get the treat is not to actually try and get it, then you should try putting two or three pieces of kibble in your hand. You may have to go through the whole routine again, because now your dog will be more tempted to get the higher-value reward.

You should also practise (with one piece of kibble again) in another room in your house, in the garden, and eventually, in a quiet area of the park. If you want to have more control of your dog everywhere you go, then you should practise this exercise everywhere you go too.

Stage two:

Ideally you will do this on the floor in your living room or kitchen, and your dog will be sitting or lying down in front of you. Show your dog the food so he is interested in it, and then place it on the floor and cover it with your hand flat over the top of it. If he isn't already, then you can encourage your dog to sniff the food. As before, he will sniff and lick your hand to get the food. Now simply repeat the exercise again and wait for him to move away and 'Leave it', and as before, reward him with a 'Good boy' the very second he moves his head away from your hand. Then say 'Take it', and remove your hand from the food.

Once he has the idea (which shouldn't take quite as long as the first time you taught him), you can introduce the eye-contact element. So 'Leave it', eye contact, 'Good boy', 'Take it', at which point you push the reward towards him so he knows he can have it.

Again, practise this lots of times in different rooms too. Don't get frustrated if your dog seems to forget everything one day and can't do the exercise. Just take it back to a step when he was doing really well, and help him to relearn what you want him to do.

It's at this time that you can go back to sitting with your dog, and start to increase the amount of time he has to wait before you say 'Take it'. Increase in very short steps. I like to count Dalmatians, believe it or not. So it would go 'Leave it', eye contact, 'Good boy' 1 Dalmatian, 2 Dalmatian, 'Take it', reward. This is going to build up his self-control in a gradual way that's fun and rewarding for him. You can and you should still talk to your dog while he's waiting for the 'Take it', so smile at him and talk and tell him what a good boy he is for waiting.

You should get some amazing focus from your dog because he will be intently watching you talk while he waits for the magical 'Take it' command to be spoken.

Stage three:

Stage three is going to make it a little more tempting for your dog. The principle is exactly the same, only this time you go from having a flat palm over the treat on the floor, and bend your fingers and shape your hand so it forms a claw-like cage over the treat. Now your dog can not only smell but also see the treat, so he may be more interested and keen to get to it than he was before.

Start the exercise by showing your dog the treat, and then place it on the floor with your hand over it in the claw position with the treat directly underneath your hand. Now wait for your dog to sniff, and then leave it and reward him when he moves his head away and looks at you. Ideally your dog will be quite good at the other 'leave its' by now, so he will quite readily move his head away because he has come to associate moving away from the treat with being rewarded.

If your dog is pawing madly at your hand or licking through your fingers to get the treat, then take it back a step and call it stage two and a half. This is where your hand partially covers the treat and is somewhere in between a flat palm and a claw shape.

Certainly I would do a couple of goes with a flat palm, just to remind my dog what the exercise is before I started doing it with a clawed hand over the treat. This just makes it a bit easier for your dog, and we always want to make it as easy as possible for the dog to learn, don't we?

Spend a few days on this stage, as the next part is harder still. Use any meal or treat times with your dog to have a practice. Do it in different rooms of the house, and then lengthen the amount of time your dog gives you eye contact before you tell him to 'Take it'.

Stage four:

This is the hardest stage and involves you leaving the treat on the floor in front of you with no hand on the treat and you just telling your dog to 'Leave it'. Have him sit or lie down before you start; then do a couple of 'leave its' with a clawed hand to get him warmed up. Then place a treat on the floor and make sure it's closer to you than it is to him. Place your hand above the treat and say 'Leave it'; then wait for some eye contact and remove your hand completely while you talk to your dog and tell him he is a good boy. Then say 'Take it' and push the treat towards him.

Repeat lots of times and gradually increase the amount of time your dog has to wait before you say 'Take it'. Repeat it in different rooms and practise outside too. Doing the exercise on different levels is another great idea, so leave the treat on the floor on a cushion, on a table or stool, or on your knee when you are sitting down – and anywhere else you can think of. This will reinforce to your dog that he should leave a treat anywhere and everywhere you want him to.

So 'leave it' is a great non-physical game that provides a mental challenge for your dog and has the added bonus that you can play it anywhere. It can also be used practically too. If you have a dog that is always picking up food (or more disgusting items) that you come across on a walk, then you can use the 'leave it' to help you distract him from doing that.

As with all our training, you need to build up somewhat to the big challenges, so don't go thinking that your dog is going to magically ignore dropped chips and half-eaten sandwiches that he finds just because you are offering a piece of his kibble as an alternative. No, we need to be a little smarter than that, and this is where stage five comes in.

Stage five:

You should start this when your dog is successfully leaving the treat on the floor as per stage four. It is essentially about getting your dog to leave the treat on the floor and rewarding him with another treat that you produce from your hand or pocket. So now you are saying to your dog 'Leave that because I have something else for you instead.'

I like to have my dog on the lead for this exercise as it gives me more control. You should have two kinds of food, and your dog should like one of them more than the other. So commence the exercise as you did in stage four; place a fairly low-value treat on the floor, and tell your dog to 'Leave it'.

Then when he gives you eye contact, show him the higher-value treat you have in your hand (make sure he has seen it; stick it under his nose if you have to). Then say his name and encourage him to come towards you and away from the treat on the floor. When he gets to you, tell him he is a good boy and give him lots of praise and finally the treat.

This is a huge lesson for a dog to learn that he can ignore and leave something that he wants but he gets rewarded even more when he does so. Practice makes perfect, so repeat this often, and vary the rewards you use too. Over time you can build up the value of the foods you use as rewards, so that the exchange more closely resembles something you would see in the park.

Once you know he has the idea, you can up the ante by maybe placing a small piece of chicken on the floor, which your dog will leave but then you reward him with two pieces and a game of his choice.

You should experiment with lots of different food inside and on walks too. If your dog is always eating things on walks that you don't want him to, then he probably won't stop until you teach him it's more beneficial for him to come and see what you have got instead. Remember dog training is a bit like reversing a car down a narrow lane. If you don't want to make a mistake, then take it slowly.

I also like to use the 'leave it' to teach a dog to stay. 'Stay' can be a difficult thing to teach especially if you are a superhero dog owner and your dog wants to be with you and follows you everywhere all the time. Why teach a 'stay' at all? I mean it's not like the old days when you could leave a dog outside of a shop you popped into. Well, truthfully you don't have to, but I think this may help if you have a dog that is reactive to other dogs, and you want to prevent flashpoint incidents from happening.

For your dog to leave something, he has to keep still and not move from the spot, which is exactly the same thing as a 'stay', isn't it? Yes, Dom, it is. So you do the exercise exactly the same as before, only now you are using the 'leave it' to keep your dog's bum glued to the floor. And I will assume that by now you have completed all the other stages and practised many times, and your dog is pretty good at leaving anything.

Find a quiet area of the park, make sure your dog is on a lead, and then get your dog's attention with the treat (or toy if you prefer). Then place the treat on the floor, and ask your dog to leave it, which he should do. Then you can reward him either with the treat on the floor and say 'Take it', or you can call your dog to you and reward him with something you have instead.

Now this time do the exercise again, and I want you to watch your dog while he is leaving the treat. You will notice that he is incredibly focused either on the treat or hopefully on you if he is waiting for you to tell him to 'Take it'. That's because you have given him a little task that focuses his attention. He isn't just sitting and doing nothing; he is actively focused on not eating the food. And if you have varied your rewards and made it really pleasurable for him to leave something, then he will get pretty good at it too. Then you will have a default exercise that you can do whenever you require your dog to sit still and ignore things that would normally distract him.

Again, don't expect your dog to start ignoring dogs or birds if he has found them very exciting for the last few years. You need to build it up slowly. So try this next time you are in the park or on a walk and you see something coming that your dog would normally be interested in. First get yourself a safe distance away so it's not too tempting for him (or cross to the other side of the road if you are walking), then take out of your pocket a tasty bit of chicken or hot dog, show it to your dog, place it on the floor in front of him, and tell him to leave it. If the treat is a high-enough-value bit of Kryptonite and you have practised the exercise lots, then your dog should focus on ignoring the food and sit still. Then when the other dog has passed by, you can reward your dog with the treat and lots of praise and affection.

Eventually you will be able to be super sneaky and just pretend to put a treat on the floor, and say 'Leave it'. Your dog will probably look quizzically at the area where you pretended to put the treat, and then you can get eye contact and encourage him to walk on with you. Then reward him as you continue your walk.

This is a little trick I learned at a puppy class I attended, and I believe they use it to help get dogs to stay still for longer periods of time as part of The Kennel Club Good Citizen Dog Scheme. The handler will pretend to put a treat on the floor in front of a dog and say 'Leave it' very quietly. Then the dog will stay put until the handler returns and rewards him. The handler passes the 'stay' test, and the dog gets rewarded for doing a 'stay'. Everyone's a winner!

Grooming Your Dog

Another low-level activity that you can do with your dog is grooming. I will be honest; over the years, I haven't done a lot of grooming with my dogs, but I do now, and the more I do it, the more I (and the dogs) enjoy it.

Obviously, because of their coats some breeds require a more intensive groom than others, but no matter how short the hair, all dogs will benefit hugely from a regular groom.

I find that grooming allows me to enjoy a few minutes just bonding with my dog. I tend to talk to him more too. (It's just like going to the hairdresser's, and your dog will love it when you tell him about your day and where you are going on holiday this year. Unless he's not invited.) I find I just get lost in the activity and spend far longer doing it than I intended, which is a good thing. In fact, studies have shown that petting and playing with your dog can significantly reduce stress hormones and elevate levels of serotonin and dopamine, which calm and relax the human. So grooming your dog is a very good thing indeed.

My good friend David Davies says his grooming sessions act as his dog's daily health check, and I love that. It's the opportunity to give your dog a check-over for any cuts, bumps, lumps, or bruises that shouldn't be there and aren't easily visible to the naked eye. Thinking of grooming this way should motivate you to do it more often too.

Grooming exercise:

If your dog isn't keen on grooming at the moment, then you can train him to enjoy it more just as you would train him to do anything else.

If your dog likes food, then you can turn part of his mealtime into a grooming session. Show your dog a piece of kibble, and with the other hand give him a little stroke or brush, and then tell him what a good boy he is, and give him the piece of kibble. Repeat this several times, gradually increasing the amount of time you spend brushing your dog. Slow down if he looks uncomfortable; remember this isn't a battle of wills, but you teaching your dog that you can enjoy grooming together.

Spend around two to five minutes doing this, and then finish and play your dog's favourite game with him. In time, he will associate the grooming with the game too and so will enjoy it more. If your dog isn't keen on being touched at the moment, then treat the whole grooming experience like a training exercise, with short sessions once or twice a day. This would be preferable to one mammoth grooming session every month.

Grooming is a great way to bring some stillness and control into a play or training session. Practising this calmness and touching your dog regularly will help you when it comes to taking him to the vet's for his yearly check-up too. Be especially gentle and doubly rewarding when you are touching sensitive areas of his body such as ears, feet, and around his bum area.

Chapter Summary

◎ Teaching your dog to 'leave it' should be high at the top of the list of things you teach him. It teaches self-control and is a mentally tiring exercise for the dog. Thinking games use up great amounts of energy, so be prepared to spend many days and weeks gradually building up the amount of time your dog can leave something. Practise the game anywhere using toys or treats, but be sure to use fairly low-value items of Kryptonite that aren't too tempting for your dog. This will help him to learn more quickly.

◎ Think about how you feel when you get all spruced up for a night out, and if someone tells you how handsome you look, your self-esteem goes into overdrive. We all like to feel good about ourselves. I'm not sure if dogs are as vain as we are, but I know they certainly appreciate being given praise. A grooming session gives you lots of opportunities to give your dog affection and tell him how much you love him. Aim to build some regular grooming sessions into your dog's routine. I groom my dogs at home but also when we are on walks too.

◎ If you are a smart cookie, you may have realised that you can combine both these low-level activities. Once your dog is regularly leaving a treat that is placed on the floor, then you can use it to make him stand still while you groom him. This puts your dog's focus onto looking at the treat and not what you are doing with the brush behind him and turns the grooming session into a training session.

CHAPTER 11
YOUR DOG'S SUPERPOWER

*"The sense of smell in all dogs is their primary doorway
to the world around them."*
– Robert Crais

My youngest son, Toby, loves superheroes. And I mean
LOVES them. His favourite are the X-Men. To explain
quickly, in case you haven't seen them... the X-Men are a
team of mutant superheroes who each have a unique power
and a super-cool name to boot, such as Storm, Cyclops,
Wolverine, and Iceman, and they are led by Professor Charles
Xavier.

In the movie *X-Men: First Class*, we go back in time to when
Charles first met and banded together the X-Men, who were
then just teenagers. They all have their powers, but they are
young and inexperienced, and they don't know how to
control them. And because of this, their powers end up
getting them into trouble. Professor X takes them under his
wing and teaches them how to control their abilities so they
can live normal(ish) lives in society with other non-mutants
(like me and you).

You shouldn't need me to tell you that your dog has some
superpowers too. There are lightning-fast Greyhounds that
can race around a track at speeds of up to 40 mph; tenacious
terriers that will dig into a rabbit hole until you pull them

out; scary-strong Staffies who can crush supposedly indestructible toys into tiny pieces; super swimmers like the Newfoundland that can glide through the water aided by their webbed feet, and crazy-intelligent Collies that seemingly work like remote-controlled dogs and can move a flock of sheep from one field to another.

But there is one superpower that all dogs share, and that is the gift of smell. Dogs possess the same five senses as us: taste, touch, smell, hearing, and sight. But, it is estimated that 30% of a dog's brain is dedicated to analysing odour, which is 40 times larger than the area that our human brains dedicate to the same task. We know for a fact that a dog's nose contains around 300 million olfactory receptors compared to our measly six million.

I love this example from Alexandra Horowitz in her book *Inside of a Dog*:

"We might notice if our coffee's been sweetened with a teaspoon of sugar; a dog can detect a teaspoon of sugar diluted in a million gallons of water: two Olympic-sized pools full."

There are dogs that can find a tiny piece of cannabis hidden inside a suitcase placed among 1000 other suitcases, and there are even dogs that are being trained to detect cancer in human beings. Medical detection dogs help alert people with diabetes when their blood sugar levels become low, which is a daily hazard for those with severe diabetes.

Now that kind of ability is not to be sniffed at…

This makes our dogs' noses around 1000 to 10,000 times better than ours, which pretty much makes your mutt an X-Dog. And a superpower like that needs careful control, otherwise your dog's nose will get him into all kinds of trouble, much like the children with superpowers in *X-Men: First Class*.

I'm sure you will be able to think of a few occasions where your dog's nose has landed him in some trouble in the past. Maybe he stole a chicken fresh out of the oven that was cooling on the top, or in the park he found a not quite empty but discarded pizza box and helped himself to what was left. He might, for example, be retrieving a ball one day when he suddenly drops it, stands stock-still and then whips his head to the left, and you both think 'Squirrel!'

We know that with all great superpowers come great responsibility – the only difference with Spider-Man is it's your dog that has the superpower and you who has the responsibility for controlling it. Playing some nose games with your dog will teach him that he can use his powers and have fun with you. To paraphrase John Rogerson, we can say control the toy, control the game, control the nose, and control the dog!

You may be thinking that you can no more influence what your dog smells than you can control what he sees. Well, that may be true, but by playing nose games regularly, you can quickly begin to control what he enjoys smelling or finding.

Teaching a 'find it'

'Find it' is a brilliant game and one I play with my dogs every single day, every walk even. Don't worry if you think your dog can't find anything; just think of it as a slower and more civilised version of a retrieve, and you will understand how easy it is. The main thing to remember is you need to have something that your dog really wants to find, so if you're in the garden or further afield, I would use a number one or two item from your dog's toys or food Kryptonite. But as with all the games we teach, you are probably better off starting this game indoors where there are fewer distractions.

Show your dog the toy and make sure he is interested enough in it to actually want it. Keep the dog on lead to stop him from getting the toy straightaway, and then you can place the toy somewhere really easy for him to find: behind a chair or cushion if you are in the house or behind a bench, tree, or bush if you are in the park. It doesn't matter if your dog sees where you put the toy at first, as he will still be using his nose. We want him to find it, remember? You need to make the finding of the toy very rewarding so he wants to do it again.

Then just encourage your dog to go and 'find it' and give him lots of praise and affection when he does. Repeat this four or five times until your dog has the idea. Then you can throw the toy behind a different thing, lead your dog a short way away from the area and then encourage him to go and find it again.

A huge mistake that almost all dog owners, including me, make with this game is that they rush ahead and try and make it too difficult by hiding the toy too far away. Then when the dog struggles to find the toy, the owner thinks he either doesn't like the game or isn't very good at it, neither of which is usually true. You are the teacher here; how fun and easy you make the finding of the toy or food will very much affect how enjoyable your dog finds the game, how quickly he learns to do it, and how much he wants to play in the future.

Find the food

You can play 'find it' using food as per the instructions above, and there are many other games you can play in the house that your dog will love playing, and you will enjoy watching him too.

You can use a baking tray or some plastic beakers to hide food under. Place five or so on the floor with a treat or some kibble under three of them, let your dog into the room, and encourage him to 'find the treats'. This is an incredibly simple game, but dogs love it, and you are encouraging your dog to use his nose.

You can start by placing a bit of food on the floor in your house. Let your dog see you do it, and then encourage him to get or 'find it'. Repeat three or four times, and then place the food behind a door or cushion, and tell your dog to 'Find it', which he will quite easily. Once your dog has the idea, you can gradually make the game more difficult. You could play the game with food already in a KONG and hide the KONG. Then your dog has to find it and work to get the food out. This is double the challenge, double the stimulation, and double the fun.

You can take this even further by placing something tasty in a KONG, then wrapping the KONG in some paper, and placing it in a small cardboard box. Your dog then has to find the box, rip the parcel open, and remove the paper to get to the KONG and the food. My Barry loves playing this game and seems to enjoy ripping up the box as much as he does finding the chicken.

It can be a great thing to do if your dog is injured and on cage rest, and you can't exercise him as much but still want to give him things to do. Some pitfalls with this game are that you need always to be present when your dog is ripping up the paper, as you don't want him ingesting any. Also, once he really gets into it, your dog won't necessarily differentiate between a box you have made and a parcel that's been put through the letter box, as I have found out to my cost once or twice...

When your dog gets good at this, then move the game out into the garden or yard and use upturned plastic plant pots to hide treats or toys under.

Just as we did with a toy, you can play the 'find the food' game in the park too. I play this game with toys and treats on a daily basis with my dogs.

Again, use a lead on your dog for control then either get him to do a 'stay' or hold the lead while you place some small bits of food over a park bench and watch your dog use his laser-guided nose to help him find the treats.

If it's safe to do so, then you can play 'sprinkles', which is just you throwing a handful of your dog's food into the grass and letting him go and find it.

Searching

Searching in this instance involves your dog trying to find you or a friend or family member. It's a great game to play when there are two or more of you exercising your dog in the park or even at home; outside is more fun though. It also helps if there are some trees big enough for a human to hide behind.

As usual I would start by playing with my dog with a toy or some food. This will help you set the scene as the park being the place where your dog plays with you.

Start with one of you holding your dog on a two-metre lead attached to his harness. (You can do this with a collar, but I think it's more comfortable for the dog to wear a harness.) The other person then plays with the dog with the toy and slowly walks away showing the dog the toy. (The dog at this point should be between the handler and hider.) The handler stands still so the dog can't move forward.

The hider then continues to move backwards and hides behind a tree or bush no more than five metres away from where the handler and dog are standing. Then as soon as the hider goes out of sight, you (the handler) encourage your dog to 'Find mammy' or 'Find Geoff' or whoever it is you are playing with. You hold the lead and just follow your dog. Take your time, as there is no rush.

Training tip:

If your dog is struggling to find the person, then they are probably hiding too far away or they haven't played enough with your dog to get him interested in the toy they have. Remember we want to make it very easy for the dog to find them and get his toy; that way he will enjoy the game and want to play again.

Repeat four or five times. If the dog is doing very well, the hider can move a little further back. Then on the fifth go, change the game a little and bring your dog's superpower into play.

This time, the hider shows the dog the toy or food as usual, but as they go behind the tree, the handler places his hand over the dog's eyes. Then when the dog is unable to see, the hider moves to a different but nearby tree (note the tree must only be a couple of metres away; we WANT the dog to find the hider!). Then when the hider is in position, the handler continues the game as before. The dog will head off as before to where he thinks the hider is, and when he gets there, he will be very surprised to find no one there.

Here is the magical part, and this is the bit where you just need to shut up and let the dog work it out. If you are very observant, you will actually see the very moment his nose kicks in and the senses switch from eyes to nose: 'Now, where is my mum?' It's important you keep schtum here, and at the very most, just encourage him with a 'Where's your mammy gone?'

At this point, your dog's nose will take over, and he will slowly but surely start sniffing the air or ground. His nose will eventually pick up the scent, and it will lead him to the hiding place, at which point everyone should go mental and tell him what a clever little doggy he is!

You can repeat this game a few times, swapping handler and hider, gradually increasing the distance, and swapping the trees you use.

Just remember to keep it nice and easy and FUN for your dog, and if he can't find the hider, you have made the game too hard for him.

Training tip:

Be careful on hot days, because any kind of nose work can be very tiring for a dog. It will also be more difficult for your dog if it's warmer, as there will be less 'scent' on the ground.

Chapter summary

- Your dog's nose is his most powerful weapon, so please use it and involve yourself in how he uses it. Anything you can do to provide an outlet for your dog's sniffing ability is going to stimulate and tire him out too. As with all the games we play, the idea is we gradually build up the drive and enjoyment of the game so we can achieve better control on walks.

- When appropriate, try and use park benches, monuments, trees, and bushes as hiding places for the toys and treats your dog finds. If you do this regularly enough, your dog will start to look forward to it. He will look to you more when you reach each stop-off point on a walk, in anticipation of his next game of 'find it'. I also think using the location like this teaches your dog that trees and benches aren't just there to wee on, but they are an apparatus for us to use in our games, which again gives you more control of your dog.

◉ Birds have to fly, bees like to buzz, and dogs have to sniff things. The more you introduce nose games into your dog's daily routine, the greater a superhero you will become to him. I guarantee you will surprise yourself how much you enjoy playing these scent games, and your dog will relish the tests too. Whether it is food, a toy, or a loved one that he is searching for, it doesn't matter; just make sure your dog finds it rewarding and enjoyable. Using exercises and games that harness the power of your dog's nose is one of the most powerful and effective ways to influence him.

CHAPTER 12
THE WORKING PET DOG

"Funny thing, employment. If you keep doing it, you keep getting paid."
– N K Jemisin

Many years ago, I was walking through my local park, and I remember seeing a man who was exercising his Collie with a ball and a ball chucker. The dog went back and forth for the ball all the time, and even when the owner let him have a breather, the dog would crouch down and lie in wait with his eyes locked on to him, just waiting to resume the game. This was way before I started my own dog business, but I remember thinking to myself, 'Why doesn't he just chill out? That must be so boring for the dog just doing that all the time.'

How very wrong I was.

See, the dog was doing a job – a pretty basic job, but one that made him very happy. Most importantly, this was a job that involved his owner. The dog's enjoyment was dependent on and came directly from the owner chucking the ball.

What is your dog's job?

I use the word 'job' as a catch-all to cover all the activities your dog can do. We know that dogs need to feel safe and they need food, interaction, and challenge. Well, now it's time to for you to provide your dog with a job that fulfils all those needs.

There are many different jobs in the world, and not every dog can or has to be a drug-finding police dog searching through hundreds of suitcases at an airport every day, or a working herder who runs dozens of miles day after day for his shepherd. So what job can your dog do?

Well, first let's define the word 'job'.

Job

1) a paid position of regular employment.
2) a task or piece of work, especially one that is paid.

The key words we need to take from that description are **paid, regular, and task.**

Your dog's job can be anything you want it to be. You just need to remember to make it a paid regular task that he ENJOYS doing.

Don't think that your dog doesn't need a job, because he definitely does. A regular series of challenges and games are essential for your dog's well-being. The challenges you provide for your dog will keep him out of trouble and help you to overcome some of the problems you are currently experiencing.

By now you should know your dog's Kryptonite. But I want you to think of the Kryptonite as being more than just the things he likes. Now you will use it to pay him for doing the things you want him to do, his wages if you like. We all like being paid with things we need and want. In our case it's money, but for your dog that tennis ball, slipper, or Yorkshire pudding is now his own personal currency.

You have already started to teach your dog some basic games and tricks using the Kryptonite as a reward. Well, that reward now becomes his payment, and now you are going to build on this by implementing a whole routine of tricks, games, and tasks that will put you at the centre of your dog's world. And you will make this very enjoyable for your dog, so he wants to do it.

You know dogs learn through repetition, so build the routine gradually, starting in a place where there are low distractions such as in your home. This way he can learn, practise, and perfect the tricks and games, before you begin to take him to locations where there are more distractions.

Once you have found something your dog likes doing, you should do it often. This gives him regular payment and will boost his self-esteem. It also increases your superhero status and gives your dog a reason to look up to you as his friend, teacher, and employer.

Dogs on the dole

We have already determined that being able to be left alone is a prerequisite for almost all pet dogs these days as most of us work (unless you take your dog with you). A dog with a job will sleep and rest or chew on a KONG while you are gone if you teach him that's what you want him to do.

Lots of my clients will complete the dog audit and start playing and having fun as I recommend; then after a week or so of this, they think *I am ready to take this show on the road.* And they head to the park where we know the dog will revert to doing the naughty thing he did before. As always, it's because they have tried to do too much too soon. I get it though; we are happiest when we are making progress, and it's natural for you to want to test your dog out to see if he is any better behaved.

To help you gradually build your dog up to going back to the park, I have set up a six-week programme in the next chapter, which any owner can follow. The programme or apprenticeship as I call it involves you using all of the games and tricks that your dog has learned so far.

Six weeks, you cry! We want things to happen quickly… I get that. We live in a world of fast food, 24-hour one-click shopping delivered to our door, TV on demand, instant this, instant that, etc. We have become accustomed to things happening straightaway.

But truly great things take time. It took Michelangelo four years to paint the Sistine Chapel. I could have painted it using some emulsion and a few rollers in less than a week. Although I doubt the Pope or any of the millions of visitors to the Vatican would have been as impressed with my efforts.

This will be the best six weeks you have ever had with your dog, and the chances are you will enjoy playing with him so much that you won't want to go to the park ever again…

Chapter summary

- Your dog's job doesn't need to be difficult at first and can just consist of a simple 'sit' and a tuggy game. Don't worry if you aren't very good at them yet; just do them anyway. You and your dog doing stuff together is all I'm bothered about for now. In time you will develop a full repertoire of tricks and games that you play with your dog.

- Remember that your dog is always learning and if you don't give him something to do, then he will find something to do anyway. That something will probably involve doing things you don't want him to do, like chasing birds or playing with dogs, chewing your furniture, or barking at the postman.

- Everyone works in our house. I'm a dog trainer, Beth is a teacher, Alex works for me and Toby does the dishes, Sidney finds toys, and Barry empties KONGs. Once you start to think of your dog as a member of the family who has to pay his way and earn everything he gets, your life with him will become so much easier.

CHAPTER 13
YOUR DOG'S APPRENTICESHIP

"A long apprenticeship is the most logical way to success. The only alternative is overnight stardom, but I can't give you a formula for that."

– Chet Atkins

So how do we train up a working pet dog? Well, we are going to start him on an apprenticeship.

The system of apprenticeships first developed in the later Middle Ages. A master craftsman was entitled to employ young people as an inexpensive form of labour, in exchange for providing food, lodging, and formal training in the craft. In this instance you are the master craftsman and your dog is the young employee.

In many jobs such as construction, engineering, and catering, this practical, on-the-job learning is the only way to learn the necessary skills and is essential if you want to be able to complete the tasks in the real world and not just in a classroom. Think about the dog that can do a brilliant 30-second stay from 10 yards away in a church hall but is unable to give his owner eye contact in a busy park. We need to find a way to move this training on so we can better manage our dog in all environments.

A human apprenticeship can last from one to four years, but I have put together a plan of action that will enable to you to bring your dog up to a good-standard working pet dog in six weeks.

There are a few caveats for you to consider before you start this programme.

1) You should first have completed your dog audit. This is a must. You can't train your dog to want to be with you and use the things you know he likes if you don't know what he likes. The dog audit process will help you to connect with your dog, and while you are playing, you will be teaching him what he has to do to please you and get the things he likes. He will learn what it takes to be a 'good boy'.

2) I set this programme to last six weeks, but that all depends on how much time you have to play with and train your dog. If you don't work and have lots of free time, then you will probably progress a lot quicker, but if you only have a set time each day to devote to your dog, then that's also fine. Just make sure the time you set aside each day is spent working through the following exercises so you play with, train, and generally have fun with your dog.

You are teaching him these tricks and games because he needs challenge in his life. And you are going to make it fun so he thinks you are a fun person to be with. But, however fast or slow your progress, you should try and avoid the place where your dog always gets into trouble, for the next six weeks. Do not, do not, and I repeat DO NOT go to the park and expect your dog to act any differently than he did previously until you have taught him something new to do.

3) I have picked out these tricks and games because I find they are easy to teach; they will help you keep your dog near you, and they are what I do with my clients' dogs and mine every day. But your dog is unique just like everyone else's. So by all means feel free to change any of the tricks or games to ones that more suit your dog. That is not to say you shouldn't try them all, and unless there is a medical reason for your dog not to do a 'spin', for example, then you should have a go. Yes, each one will be difficult at first, but that's the challenge we are looking for. So take your time and enjoy the learning.

4) I've touched on this already, but please remember to make it FUN for your dog. You will see we start off all the tricks and games at home and then gradually increase the repertoire of things he can do over time. And as we start each new trick, you practise the one you have just taught in a different location. This is like learning to run and adding another half-mile each time you train. Yes, it may be only another three minutes' jogging, but these increases are achievable and manageable, and as you tick off each milestone, you feel good about yourself, and you keep going.

5) Whenever you use food rather than a toy, make sure it is a low-value food from your list of favourite foods. You should really just use your dog's daily food allowance and spread it out over the course of the day. Do not feed your dog too much food or too many tasty treats, or by week four your dog may well have doubled in size. We want a dog with a fit mind and a fit body too.

6) Read that quote again at the start of the chapter. We all learn best by doing and that means making mistakes too. But I really urge you to have a go at these easy tricks. Don't think that trick training or game playing is something that only dog trainers or other people do. Teaching your dog something new really brings you closer together, and it feels good too.

So without further ado, here is an apprenticeship programme your dog can start straightaway.

The six-week play programme

Week one:

Play every day… well for the first five days anyway.

Seriously, I want you to get on the floor and play with your dog. Complete the dog audit and find out your key five things for each category. This is very easy to do and should be lots of fun for both of you.

Location – home, sitting room, and dining room.

Depending on how serious the issues you are having with your dog are, I would recommend keeping walks to a minimum for this week. Maybe just go out for toileting and maybe a brisk walk to finish off a play session, but try and completely avoid taking your dog to places you know he is going to find it difficult not to react to whatever sets off his bad behaviour.

Be sure to make any play sessions fun and enjoyable for your dog. If you haven't played much in the past, then this may not be very easy for you at first, but stick with it because it will get much easier in time. Go back to the dog audit and complete all the exercises so you have a full list of your dog's Kryptonite.

If you have a dog that is already very playful and even a bit overbearing, then you should move quickly on from playing to getting his attention and making him work harder, by teaching him the tricks he has to do to get the rewards he desires.

Day six and seven or sooner, start introducing the super six tricks in order – 'sit', 'down', 'spin', 'catch it', 'through the legs' and 'leave it'. Use ASTR as your guide to help you do this. Get your dog's ATTENTION then SHOW him what you want him to do by luring him into position with his Kryptonite, and REWARD him with it when he does it. Once he has got the idea, you can add the command and TELL him what it is he is doing, and then reward him. Remember to reward quickly and appropriately and supplement the actual Kryptonite with lots of affection and praise.

You should be using a low-value item of Kryptonite – a number four or five from your list.

Week two:

PLAY

Continue to play with your dog (or interact if you have a heart of stone and can't bring yourself to play), and make every session fun by playing tuggy, 'fetch', and 'find it' games. You will quickly see which game your dog likes the most. It is usually the one he is best at, but continue to play all three games, because the more games he enjoys, the more your dog will want to be with you. Keep praising him for giving you eye contact, and turn every meal or treat time into an opportunity to get your dog to do something for you.

Start playing games in your garden or yard, and then move to a very quiet area near where you live. You will find playing outside more difficult than inside, so keep mixing up the Kryptonite you use until you find something your dog loves outdoors. More importantly, you need to increase your enthusiasm when playing outside. If it's too difficult to get your dog's attention, then move back inside and stick to indoors for another week.

By now, you should be pretty good with the first trick, so start to fade out actually holding the Kryptonite when you lure your dog. For example, if you were practising a 'sit', you may still use the Kryptonite to get his ATTENTION, but then maybe just SHOW him with an empty hand movement (i.e. the same raised hand movement you did with the

Kryptonite in your hand but now with no Kryptonite), and at the same time TELL him to sit. As soon as he does it, say 'Good boy' and *then* give him the reward from your pocket, as well as lots of praise and affection.

You should now start practising a 'sit' in other rooms and also in your yard or garden (where you may need to go back to luring with the Kryptonite again). Your dog won't necessarily sit straightaway outside, and you may have to reteach him how to do it. Don't get frustrated at your dog if he doesn't know. He's not being awkward; he genuinely doesn't know what you want him to do, so SHOW him again. Start off with a game to get his attention, and build up his excitement and desire for the Kryptonite. Once you have some focus, begin luring him into a 'sit' with lots of praise and affection. You may have to repeat the teaching of each exercise every time you go to a new location.

This week you should also start a new trick in your sitting room. So next on the list is a 'down'. You should go back and follow the instructions for this on page 151. Again take your time and don't get frustrated if your dog doesn't do this as well he did the 'sit'. It's a new exercise, so be patient.

Training exercises for week two:

Continue practising the 'sit' (reducing the lure and the hand signal) in the sitting room and teach and practise the 'sit' in the kitchen, dining room, and garden (or any rooms your dog is allowed in).

Begin teaching a 'down' in the sitting room, using ASTR and the instructions for the exercise from chapter 9.

Play with your dog and have fun!

Did I mention you should be having fun??

Week three:

This week you can add a 'spin' to the repertoire and continue practising 'sit' and 'down' in other locations. Continue to make this fun for your dog, and after five or six attempts, finish the session with a game your dog likes or give him three or four treats. Reflect on what went well and how happy your dog looks. Do you feel like you are connecting with him more? Hopefully, the answer to this question will be yes!

Training exercises in week three:

Teach a 'spin' in the sitting room using ASTR and follow the instructions on how to teach your dog the exercise on page 154.

Continue to practise 'down', reducing the lure (in the sitting room) and using the Kryptonite as required in the kitchen and dining room.

Continue to practise the 'sit' in the yard or garden but without any hand signal now. See how quietly you can say 'Sit' and still get your dog to do it.

Begin practising the 'sit' regularly on any walks you do outside as well. Set yourself a target of a 'sit' with good eye contact before you cross every road or after every three lamp posts if you are walking on a single stretch of path. The point is you should be engaging with your dog outside as much as you do inside. Be sure to reward him with a treat at first (much easier than using a toy on a busy path) but also lots of praise and affection.

Remember, at the moment your dog will associate being outside with having fun that doesn't involve you, so start off small and begin to get him used to looking at you and sitting.

Week four:

PLAY

Teach a 'twist' in the sitting room using ASTR. If you remember, a 'twist' is just a 'spin', but the other way round. Once again, don't just assume your dog will do this easily. To your dog it's a completely different exercise to a 'spin', although by now hopefully your dog is enjoying learning something new to get a reward or a game that he likes playing.

Practise the 'spin' in the kitchen, hall, and dining room. Practise a 'down' outside in the yard or garden fading the lure so it is just a hand movement.

Down to a 'sit':

You can also practise going from a 'down', back up to a 'sit'. This can be harder than you think, so don't rush it.

When your dog is in the 'down' position, get his ATTENTION with a toy or treat and then SHOW him what to do by very slowly moving your hand straight up from his nose. As with all the tricks, you need to take tiny baby steps at first and reward him for moving up a little bit. Wait until he is almost fully in a 'sit' before you REWARD him.

Continue practising the 'sit' when you are out and about on walks too, and ask your dog to 'Sit' each time you pass every other lamp post. Keep this light and fun; if you act like you are enjoying it, there is more chance your dog will too. Start practising a 'down' on walks too. Find a quiet area away from traffic, people, and cars, get his attention with a toy or treat as you did in the house, and then lure him into a 'down' using ASTR. You may need to increase the Kryptonite and choose a number three from your list. Some dogs don't like the wet floor or lying on grass, so don't stress if he doesn't want to do it. You want him to enjoy the training and see it as being fun.

Week five:

By now you should be quite proficient with all of the tricks you have taught in weeks one to four, and your dog will be getting pretty good at some of them too. Not only that, but he may also be anticipating what he thinks you want him to do; dogs are crafty little buggers.

Be careful here that your dog doesn't start training you by just jumping into a 'sit' or a 'down' before you even ask him to and then automatically expecting a treat, a cuddle, or a 'Good boy.'

Well, OK he can have a 'Good boy' for doing it, as it is something we have trained him to do. But if he does a 'sit', then you should ask him for a 'down' or a 'spin'. If he jumps into a 'down', then ask him to come back up to a 'sit'. This isn't you being awkward; it's just you keeping the challenge going for him. Working dogs especially seem to respond better the more things you give them to do, but any breed can learn multiple tricks. You could try doing one of these:

- Teach a 'catch it' in the sitting room using ASTR
- Practise a 'twist' in the kitchen and dining room
- Practise a 'spin' in the garden
- Start to incorporate 'down' on your walks before you cross a road
- Practise a 'sit' off lead or on a long lead in a quiet area of the park

Week six:

Now you can start mixing the tricks up into a combination of tricks. Ask your dog to do a 'sit', into a 'down', and back up to a 'sit'. Then take a step back so he moves towards you, and direct him into a 'spin' and then a 'twist' before you ask him to sit again. Throw him the treat to finish with a perfect 'catch it'. Ta-daaaah! Now you are really motoring, and we can start to build a routine of tricks.

- Teach a 'through the legs' in the sitting room. Again use your little friend ASTR to help you and follow the instructions for this on page 156
- Practise 'catch it' in the kitchen and dining room
- Practise 'twist' in the garden
- Practise 'spin' along with 'down' and 'sit' on your walks, and as above, start to build a routine of tricks that you can do outside too

Et voila, you now have an easy plan you can follow to train your dog and teach him some new tricks and games to play with you.

You don't have to do this in six weeks, far from it. This is just a template to follow, but you may complete it in a shorter or longer period of time. I would suggest you have the first four games and tricks (tuggy, retrieve, 'leave it', and 'find it') locked down, so you can command a good focus from your dog before you move onto the park area.

What matters is you have a plan to follow, so if the exercises I set in weeks one and two actually take you a month to perfect, that is not a problem. Far better you do that and have lots of fun along the way than try and rush through to week six in 10 days. Then you are likely to have a disaster in the dog park when your dog doesn't want to play with you because he would much rather sniff that Spaniel's bum.

A marathon not a sprint

I've never done a marathon, but I have done a half-marathon and that was hard enough. I talked about doing the Great North Run for years and finally put my name down when my friend Chris and I decided we would do it together. I was dreading starting those first few runs, but we followed a training plan where we ran three times a week and added a minute or two each time we went out. It was still hard at first, but not the nightmare I thought it was going to be. Within a month we were up to running for 15 minutes without stopping, and five months later, I recorded a fairly respectable 1 hour 54 for the GNR. Run, Forrest, run!

Keep your training sessions short and sweet too. Ten minutes is plenty to start with, and you can increase the time as you progress. If you find yourself really struggling with a trick, then take a step back and think how you can make this easier for your dog. Is the treat or toy you are using too stimulating for your dog or not rewarding enough? If so, change the reward. Is the environment too distracting? Dogs sometimes struggle to concentrate when they change locations, so take a step back and practise indoors for another few days.

Feel free to change any of these tricks to ones that more suit your dog or ones that you prefer to do. For example, your dog may start to lift one of his paws while he is in a 'sit'. Brilliant, you can teach him a 'high five' as well. When you begin to teach your dog to go from a 'down' up to a 'sit', you may find he begins to edge towards you while lying on the floor. Well, that's the start of teaching a crawl, so go with that if you wish.

Be flexible and enjoy it; the more you praise and reward your dog for having a go, the more he will want to please you.

Whatever tricks you use at the start, make sure they are the ones you continue to practise and lock down in each of the locations, so if you do a 'high five' instead of a 'spin', then do a 'high five' in the kitchen, garden, and out on a walk too. This enables you to measure your own progress.

Chapter summary

◎ Teaching your dog new tricks is never a waste of time. Don't just think of it as a trick. You are giving your dog a challenge and a purpose in life. Most dog owners teach a 'sit' and 'high five' if the dog is lucky, but you are not most dog owners. Superhero dog owners are their dog's friend and teacher for life. Superhero dog owners are the ones whose dogs love learning things with mammy and daddy, especially if it means they get to enjoy all their items of Kryptonite.

◎ This six-week programme will give you something to focus on while you are avoiding the things that normally set off your dog's bad behaviour.

◎ The dogs and owners that play together stay together. Jeez, that's a bit cheesy isn't it, even for me. But it's also true, so I'm leaving it in there!

CHAPTER 14
YOUR DOG IN THE COMMUNITY

The Tom and Jerry effect

One of the unexpected pleasures of having children was the opportunity to experience all my favourite Disney childhood movies, like *The Jungle Book* and *Dumbo*. Both Alex and Toby have always enjoyed cartoons, and I remember when my Alex (now 19) had grown out of Teletubbies and Postman Pat but was too young for The Simpsons we used to watch Tom and Jerry cartoons over and over again.

In some of the episodes, the human who owned Tom the cat (you only ever saw her feet and ankles) would tell Tom before she left that he must be a good boy and not make any mess. As soon as she left, Jerry the mouse would show up and would indeed cause all kinds of mischief. In some of the cartoons, Tom would look at Jerry and start imagining him nestled in a sandwich or roasting on a spit. At that moment a little angel version of Tom would appear on his shoulder and say 'Now Thomas, remember you have to be a good cat and leave the mouse alone.' Tom would start to listen to the angel cat, only for the little devil version of Tom to appear on the other shoulder and remind him how much he loves the taste of mouse and that no one would ever know if he had just a teeny tiny bite of him.

Inevitably the 'Bad Tom' would win the actual Tom over, and he would ignore his conscience and go after Jerry, who he never caught obviously, much to Alex's amusement and mine.

This little story highlights the situation your dog will find himself in when you begin taking him back out into the big wide world. By now you will have spent several weeks (hopefully six) bonding and playing with your dog using toys, treats, and affection, and you should be an expert in using these things to train him.

So one day you go to the park, and you are having great fun practising your new tricks. You have just sent your dog off to find a ball when at the other end of the park you see another dog coming around the corner.

Your dog also clocks the other dog, and you immediately call him back, but instead of heading straight back to you, he freezes for a second and thinks. Unseen by you, on one shoulder appears an angel dog that tells your dog that he really should come back to you because you have toys and treats and you love him very much. Your dog thinks about this, but then on the other shoulder appears the devil dog. The devil dog implores your dog to go over and see the other dog and reminds him how much fun he always has when he does that.

And that, dear reader, is the Tom and Jerry effect.

This is quite a conundrum for your dog, isn't it? On the one hand (or shoulder) he has the option of doing the right thing, which is coming back to you, and on the other hand he has the option of the bad thing, which is running away from you to play with a dog, chase a pigeon, or roll in fox shit.

Of course, we are assuming here that your dog knows the right thing to do. At first he won't. To him there is no correct and incorrect option to choose from; there is only the one he wants to do or the one that is the most enjoyable to him. Another way to put it would be to say the one he is <u>allowed</u> to do. And it's your job to make sure that your dog isn't allowed to do the naughty thing and is given a better option instead.

Make it easy on yourself

Here's a simple rule for you to follow when you are considering letting your dog off lead but are worried that you may lose control.

When you are just about to let him off lead, is he looking at you? Is he waiting in anticipation of a game with his favourite piece of Kryptonite or is he straining at the leash to chase a bird, say hello to someone's kids, or go and find one of his doggy friends? If he is interested in what he is looking at and it's not you, then keep him on the lead.

Is there anything nearby that could distract him and cause you to lose control? If so, then keep him on a long lead or move to a quieter area of the park where there are no distractions.

You need to be completely honest with yourself about your own dog's behaviour. If you have a dog that has never really played with other dogs, then another dog coming over is not going to have much appeal.

But if your dog has played with dogs a lot in the past and enjoyed it, then the task will be much more difficult, and it is highly likely that even if you intervene quickly, he will run off to see the other dog. Why? Because he's a dog and given half the chance he will seek out the thing he enjoys doing.

This may be even truer of dogs who as puppies attended puppy parties, where they were joined together in a 'training class' and encouraged to play with the other puppies. In the same class they may well have practised some basic obedience and some tricks, but what do you think will be the strongest memory and connection they will associate with that class? Will it be learning a 'sit' and a 'leave it' with their owner, or the play session where they got to grab and chase the other puppies? Dogs are always learning, and puppies are like sponges.

Not all puppy classes are like that. The one I attended with Sid, my Cocker, placed the emphasis firmly on the OWNER playing with his puppy. So if you have a puppy, my advice would be to check thoroughly what is being taught at any potential puppy class in your area, and I would definitely ask 'Do you allow or encourage the puppies to play with each other in class?' If the answer is yes, even if just for 10 minutes, then avoid this like the plague. Far better you don't attend a puppy class and just train your puppy yourself than take him to a class where the most enjoyable thing he learns is that other dogs are for playing with.

Of course, this advice is only applicable if you want an easy life with your dog. If you want drama and you think you will enjoy chasing your dog around the park, then by all means go ahead. Remember your dog can't unlearn existing behaviour traits; you can only try and teach him new ones. It is far better for him to learn that other dogs and puppies are just things that exist and that he will encounter them on walks much like people, buses, lamp posts, and lollipop ladies, etc. So teach him they are nothing to be afraid of, but they are nothing to get excited about either.

Taking the lead

One thing you can do to stop your dog ignoring you is to use a wonderful invention called a dog lead.

You should consider investing in a long lead of five or 10 metres, or you could just use an old washing line if you wish. At the very least, use a two- metre training lead you can let trail on the floor. The lead is a safety net that you can hold onto or stand on and stop your dog from ignoring you.

By using a training lead, you completely take the decision-making out of your dog's hands, and you prevent him from making the same mistake again.

This is why I recommend you complete the exercises in the book in the correct order.

By now you have spent many hours playing lots of games with your dog, you will have built up a huge reserve of happy experiences, and you have told him on thousands of occasions that he is a good boy.

The bank of experiences is going to come in really handy now. As you hold onto that lead, you hopefully won't be experiencing the terror you may have done before you started this training. Because now you are a superhero dog owner, he won't bolt for it (well, he won't be able to because he's on the lead), but now you can also call his name in that cheery voice you have been practising every day. And if you have rewarded each name call with something pleasant, then your dog will more readily look at you. And once he is looking at you, then you know you have his attention and you can tell him he is a good boy.

Once you have his attention, you can take out one of his favourite toys or treats, which he further associates with fun, and you can lead him away from the distraction. Then when you are a fair distance away, you can have a short game with him and tell him what a good boy he is.

Remember prohibition? You can't ban fun for your dog, but you need to provide a different outlet for him instead, one that you can control. In time, your dog will look to you more for fun and entertainment, but in the meantime, while he is still completing his apprenticeship and learning the new routine, you need to be able to control him by keeping him on a lead.

So how do you know when he is ready to be let off lead and given more freedom? Well, you test him, of course.

Turning tricks into tests

By now you have a nice routine of tricks and games that you can mix and match into various combinations. And if you have followed the six-week programme, then you will also have been gradually exposing your dog to the outside world as you practise tricks in your sitting room, kitchen, and garden and then on walks. And like me you will have discovered that it's a lot harder to train a dog outside than it is inside. But if you have kept at it, over time you will realise that even though it's more difficult, if you have the right toys and treats and you put enough effort into the exercise, then yes, you can indeed get your dog to focus on you enough to perform his little routine of tricks.

By the end of the six-week training programme, you haven't just taught your dog a few tricks and games; you have taught him a whole new way of enjoying life by sharing activities that involve you. He will have less need for any of the things on the 'Bad Kryptonite' list, because he has you to provide fun, entertainment, and challenge in his life.

Well, now you can use your routine of tricks as a barometer to test how focused your dog is on you. You may have been doing this subconsciously already, but it's time to bring everything you have been working on to the fore.

Let's say the big problem you were having was that your dog was too reactive to other dogs and was always running away from you. The next time you walk by your local park and you see some dogs playing together on the other side of the fence, just stop and see how he reacts. If he looks at the dogs and then back at you when you say his name, you know all those times rewarding him with eye contact will have been worth it. You could then ask him to do a 'sit' and then a 'down' and a 'spin'. If he manages all three, very well done, you have done a great job bonding with him, and you are ready to take it to the next step.

I would try this same scenario another couple of times, and then move a little closer to someone who is walking their dog. You could even get on the same side of the field as them but have your dog on a long lead. Repeat the trick test and run through your routine; make it lots of fun for your dog and play the games he loves. When you do this, you are teaching your dog that he can and should have fun with you EVEN if there are other dogs around.

If you tried this and your dog was immediately pulling on the lead or whining because he wanted to get to the dog in the distance, then you know straightaway that it would be a waste of time even to attempt taking your dog closer. He clearly isn't ready to be off lead near other dogs yet, and the temptation to run off and play would be too great. This isn't a failure on your part and just means you should take a couple of steps back and go back to playing away from any distractions.

It is likely you will end up somewhere in between those two extremes at first, with your dog eventually focusing on you, but still somewhat interested in certain dogs he sees. It's your job as a responsible dog owner to continue to play with, train, and test your dog until you are satisfied he is sufficiently interested in you and giving you good focus almost all of the time before you consider letting him off lead. Even when you are very satisfied, I would still use a long lead for another month or so, as a safety net.

In the above instance where the dog was too reactive, I would place special emphasis on practising recalls so your dog is constantly having it reinforced that when he comes back to you good things happen. But you can use the tricks and tests method to help you with any other issues you may be having too.

If your dog always jumps up at people, you should make doing a 'sit' or a 'down' the main exercise you work on, so that becomes his default position whenever you are training him.

For dogs that bark at the front door, you should make going to his bed the default position, as this will keep him away from the door. Duh! I know it sounds obvious doesn't it, but until you are told you probably wouldn't have thought of that as a solution. So treat your dog for sitting on his bed. Lure

213

him onto it if you have to, and then in time you can add 'In your bed' or a more original command if you feel the need.

Your dog and the law

In July 2007, the UK government successfully passed a smoking ban in public places. The law banned smoking in pubs, bars, restaurants, etc.

And if smokers wanted to smoke, they had to stand outside in the rain.

I'm not judging smokers here, as I believe in free choice. However, I'm as aware as the next man that smoking or breathing in someone else's smoke is bad for you, so I didn't lament the ban coming in, even though I worked for a tobacco company at the time.

In fact, it was smokers who were responsible for smoking being banned in the first place. Why? Because as long as they were allowed to smoke wherever they wanted, they did so, and there was a section of the smoking population who just didn't care about how their actions were affecting those who didn't smoke. And people who choose not to smoke quite rightly didn't want to have to wave smoke away from their faces in a bar, have fag ash land on a meal, or go home smelling like ashtrays.

Yes, there are always busybodies that live for complaining and overzealous governments which can't wait to justify their existence and create new laws that restrict our freedom, but smokers didn't half make it easy for them to do that.

Well, if it was the smokers that caused smoking to be banned, then it is irresponsible dog owners that will determine how much freedom dogs will be allowed in public places in the future. Dog control orders and the banning of dogs from certain public parks is becoming a hot issue, and already there are many areas of the UK where you can't exercise a dog off leash. I fear this will only increase over time, and it will be irresponsible dog owners who make this happen sooner.

Yes, accidents happen all the time, nobody is perfect, and I too have been thoroughly ashamed of things my dogs have done in the past. But if I analyse it, then I guess I'm more ashamed of the things I have let my dogs do. Because it's not the dog's fault; it's mine! And in your community you are the personal representative for dog owners all over the world (and for future generations of dog owners too).

To focus your mind on the task, let's quickly take a look at the Dangerous Dogs Act in the UK.

The Dangerous Dogs Act in the UK currently states that it is against the law to let any dog (of any breed) be dangerously out of control anywhere, such as:

- In a public place
- In a private place, e.g. a neighbour's house or garden
- In the owner's home

Out of control

Your dog is considered dangerously out of control if it:

◎ Injures someone

◎ Makes someone worried that it might injure them

A court could also decide that your dog is dangerously out of control if either of the following applies:

◎ It attacks someone's animal

◎ The owner of an animal thinks they could be injured if they tried to stop your dog attacking their animal

In addition, a farmer is allowed to kill your dog if it's worrying their livestock.

Even with just this brief overview, you can see the importance of keeping a dog under control. The next stage for this kind of law could be outright banning of dogs in public places. So let's protect our right to own and enjoy a dog by making sure that our dogs are under control at all times and they are something that everyone in our community can enjoy. Even from a distance.

We started this chapter by talking about responsibility and having better control of your dog off lead. But I used to struggle walking my dog even when he was on lead, so let's look at what I did to remedy that.

How to stop pulling on the lead

You may be wondering why, when we are approaching the final section of the book, am I only now covering pulling on the lead. Well, it's for a very good reason. Dogs pull on the

216

lead because it works. Each time they pull, they move forward and get a little closer to the park, which is full of exciting things to explore.

Despite what certain dog whisperers would have you believe, you can't just take a deep breath, be calm and assertive, and expect your dog to stop pulling on the lead just like that. Especially if it's something he has done for a long time. But you know better than that, don't you…?

Let's be honest here though, stopping your dog from pulling on the lead isn't as easy as teaching a 'sit' or a 'down' or even a retrieve. Dogs are strong, and the very nature of walking your dog means you are coming into contact with new sights and smells every few metres. So if your dog is a puller, then he is being rewarded for pulling you along, as with each pull he gets closer to the park or the next lamp post.

To stop a dog pulling on the lead, you need him to be looking at you and not have his nose pressed to the pavement. It's much easier to get his attention and focus if you have first worked through all the exercises in the book. If you do this, then your dog will have many more reasons and will more readily give you eye contact on a walk.

Trying to train your dog not to pull without first getting his attention will be much more difficult and will lead to you feeling frustrated at telling your dog off all the time.

I understand that you still have to walk your dog, so in this section I will share with you my three-point plan so you can teach your dog not to pull, but at the same time allow you to walk him without the walk degenerating back into the tug of war it currently is.

Three-point plan to stop pulling on the lead:

The first is to stop making pulling on the lead rewarding for your dog. I would recommend you use some kind of gentle head collar. On its own, it won't stop your dog from pulling altogether, but it will make your dog much easier to control than if he has the lead attached to a collar or a harness. More control means you can manage your dog better and then still walk with him at a brisk pace and get some good exercise without getting stressed and pissed off because he is pulling your arm out all the time. You aren't teaching your dog anything new here; you are just making it harder for him to pull. However, I find it gives you much more control. So using a lead like this allows you to manage the situation rather than fix it.

The second thing you should to do to make life a little easier is to wear your dog out **before** you take him out. Yeah, I know you think that the walk is going to do that, but in all honesty, it isn't. If your dog is a working breed or any kind of dog that is high energy, then a 20-minute walk on the lead is only going to act as a warm-up.

Playing with your dog before you leave the house will take the edge off him and mean he has slightly less energy to pull you along. You have lots of games you can play with your dog now, so choose the one that tires him the quickest. As well as getting rid of some excess energy, playing with your dog will get him more interested in you so should make it easier for you to keep his focus when you are walking.

So using a head collar and wearing him out pre-walk should have a big effect on your walks. If you want to teach your dog to walk happily beside you, then the next step is the hardest, and you need to practise regularly and consistently to be successful.

Heelwork is now often referred to as loose lead walking, and I quite like that expression, as it's not really necessary to have your dog walk exactly to heel with his head pressed against your thigh as in competition heelwork. The idea is you make it more pleasurable for him to want to be beside you than it is to be in front of you pulling. And as always we can use ASTR to help us.

Get your dog's ATTENTION with the Kryptonite and then SHOW him what you want him to do by luring him into a heel position beside you. Get the toy or treat and put it under his nose, and literally lure him into position. Imagine the toy is attached to a very short piece of string that is attached to your dog's nose. Slowly trace a half-circle away from your body and round behind you, so your dog follows and ends up alongside you; then say 'Good boy' and give him the treat. Repeat this lots, and when he has the idea, you can start adding the TELL as he gets into position.

Once he is doing that, you can take a step forward. At the same time, talk to your dog and try and keep him lured in the heel position with a treat in your left hand (if your dog is on the left). As he gets better, you can gradually add more steps.

The main thing to remember is to reward the dog only when he is in the heel position. You are teaching him that he gets rewarded for being beside you, in just the same way you taught him a 'sit' or a 'down' or a 'through the legs'.

Chapter summary

◎ Being a responsible dog owner is way more fun than it sounds. And once you have taken the time really to get to know your dog, you won't want to share him with anyone else anyway. The law doesn't care if your dog is friendly or not, so always be the fun and try to keep his attention on you.

◎ When you move from the relative safety of your house and garden, then you need to step up the control. Take all the decision-making out of your dog's hands, and try never to put him in a position where he can make a mistake. Remember the Tom and Jerry effect. Your dog will choose whatever is more appealing to him, so don't let him off lead until you are sure that is you.

◎ Remember the lead is your safety net, so buy one and use it. I like to use a shorter two-metre lead, as my dog is so close it almost forces me to interact with him. You should practise using a lead on your dog while you play with him at home and in the garden, so you get used to handling him using one arm in the park. Your dog will also get used to the fact that being on a long lead means he still has fun with you.

CHAPTER 15
THE HUNGER GAMES

"Hounds follow those who feed them."
— Otto von Bismarck

I have dedicated this short chapter exclusively to your dog's food because it's a very precious resource that most dog owners can use more effectively, to make living with their dogs much easier. Let's find out why...

Go back in time by around 30,000 years to when men lived in caves. Let's imagine that over a particular few days, a tribe successfully hunted a mammoth. They used almost all parts of the mammoth, but there were still a few pieces left over. On the outskirts of a cave there were some wild dogs or wolves who had been taking a keen interest in the goings-on at the cave. Some of them had been venturing closer to the humans and occasionally were rewarded with some scraps.

Now expert opinion differs on how exactly humans and wolves came together, but it isn't hard to imagine a scenario where man may have come upon a stray or abandoned wolf cub and raised it within his family. This semi-domesticated wolf would in time have taken a place at the hearth and taken on the role of hunter and guarder as well as companion, but it was food that brought man and wolf together.

You should know by now that I am a huge fan of training your dog through play and interaction, using toys and affection to help you bond with him and reward him. I go on about playing with your dog because most dogs just love playing; they crave attention, excitement, and entertainment, and if we don't provide it, then they will find it elsewhere.

You certainly won't be as important to your dog if you just use food to train him. What happens if you just train with food, and one day at the park your little Schnauzer finds a scent that leads him to a rather attractive female, and before you know it, the dogs are frolicking around like a scene from *Lady and the Tramp*? You try and call him over and stand with your bit of cheese, but your dog thinks 'Actually, I'm not hungry, Dad. You can have that bit. I will stay here.'

It's a much better idea to have your dog think you are an exciting person to be with rather than just a food dispenser. Think of it as you providing dinner and a show rather than just a pizza takeout.

You should try and inject lots of emotion into your training even when you are using treats. Dogs love attention, and by giving your dog a smile and a stroke and telling him he is a good boy, you are giving him a much more personal reward than just the treat. Training this way will mean that in time you may be able to phase the treats out and just use your voice and your affection as rewards for your dog.

All that aside, it has to be said that for most dogs, food is their number-one pleasure. And there are ways you can use your dog's food a lot better than just feeding two meals a day and a few treats. And if you currently just leave your dog's food down all day for him to graze on, then in my humble and correct opinion, this is a waste of what for many dogs is their most precious resource. Think back to when you did the dog audit and I recommended that you stopped leaving your dog's favourite toys lying around the house and kept them for when you were playing with him. It's a similar thing with the food. You won't be able to get your dog to work for his food if it's a free resource he can have whenever he wants.

If there were bags of money in the foyer of your office block that you were allowed to help yourself to on a Monday morning, would you walk past them and still go to work, or just help yourself and blow off the pointless task of actually earning it?

We have already discussed using food to teach your dog tricks, and if you are struggling to get your dog interested in a toy, then using food to play with, train, and entertain your dog may be your only option. It's worth stressing that if you are going to use food, you should only use the regular amount of food your dog eats throughout the day and not just feed more when you do any training with him. If you have to use a higher-value treat, then be aware of how many calories that treat will have, and adjust your dog's daily food intake accordingly.

You can get more out of your dog's daily intake by spreading his food out into several portions, but don't start taking food away from your dog and putting him in a situation where he feels like he has to defend his food. Far better for your dog to see you as the giver of food and the provider of nice things that he likes, and leave any macho food-bowl standoffs for dog whisperers who enjoy being bitten.

So instead of giving your dog his whole breakfast or tea in one bowl, you could split it into five portions and use it as a reward for a simple recall exercise; you can put a small amount of food into your dog's bowl then walk away from him, and when he is finished, call him to you in a nice cheery voice and reward him with a handful of meal. Repeat this four or five times, always being sure to supplement the giving of the food with praise and affection.

I split my own dogs' daily ration of food and treats into thirds. One third is split between two small meals, one in the morning and one in the evening.

The second portion is spread throughout the day and fed by hand in various games and training exercises – some goes in my coat pocket to use when I'm at the park, and some is placed in a bowl that goes on my mantlepiece to use indoors either as part of training or just to reinforce any good behaviour my dogs might exhibit throughout the day.

The final third I use in food dispensers, which entertain my dogs throughout the day when I am busy doing other things. Depending on how busy I am, I may even split the whole day's ration so I train with half of it and the rest will go in food dispensing toys. I am going to go into the wonderful world of food dispensing toys next, but see how I use my dog's food throughout the whole day to train, entertain, and challenge him. Would your dog enjoy his food a little more if he has to earn it rather than just be given it as one or two meals to graze on whenever he pleases?

Food games

Dogs rarely seem to get bored when it comes to finding food, and if you wish, you should be able to get your dog to find a whole bowl's worth of kibble even if it's fed in individual pieces. You can play 'find it' games with your dog's food in your house, hiding pieces under upturned cups, or from one room to another, outside in the garden, and even in your local park. Be careful outside that your dog doesn't leave any treats behind or eat anything else that could be dangerous for him. The instructions for teaching a 'find it' game can be found on page 178,

You also have the 'leave it' and the 'catch up' games that you should use to mentally and physically tire your dog out. However, there is another way you can challenge your dog further with food even when you are not at home.

King KONG

Most dog owners I meet own a KONG toy, but few use them to their full potential. In case you live on the moon, KONGs are funny-shaped food dispensers that are made from super-tough rubber. Most dogs struggle to chew them to pieces, which makes them incredibly safe and perfect for putting food in. The standard one is the red KONG, but there is also a black version, which is even tougher for dogs with super-strong jaws. There are also softer puppy KONGs and a purple version for older dogs whose jaws may not be so strong. I also own a number of Planet Dog treat dispensers too, and my dogs have lots of fun with both.

Of course, you could just use an empty milk carton. Rinse it out, throw the top away and fill with some treats or kibble and give to your dog. He will probably have great fun exploring how to get the food out of it. Barry seems to really enjoy ripping up boxes, and he has become quite the expert at it too. But the problem with using something like that is you really need to observe your dog all the time in case he rips off a piece of cardboard or worse, plastic, and tries to eat it.

That's why I recommend buying several food dispensing toys that have been made for dogs. There are loads on the market to choose from; the ones above are just my personal favourites. More important than the treat dispenser is you actually using it. Dogs love sniffing, licking, and chewing, so by providing them with a suitable toy crammed with food, you are providing an outlet and a further challenge that you can build into your dog's daily routine.

There are a million ways to fill a treat dispenser, and as you already know your dog's five favourite foods you should have no trouble filling one to your dog's satisfaction. You can fill the toy with 10% favourite treat and 90% regular kibble, and your dog will still love the KONG. The challenge of getting to the tasty stuff inside will bring him a lot of joy, so be creative with what you put inside the treat dispenser. If you don't have one, then go and buy one, and if you already have one, then get a different kind. Providing you wash them between uses, you can use them over and over again so they are great value for money, and if your dog could, then he would thank you for it too.

Chapter summary

◉ There are a number of dog trainers out there who would have you believe you shouldn't just use food when you are training a dog. I agree with that. You should always use emotion and praise in addition to the food you are using to reward your dog. Food rates pretty high on most dogs' wish list, so you would be silly not to use it.

◉ Use it all throughout the day too. Use it to practise tricks or retrieves or 'find it' games. Use it in KONGs as often as your dog will eat from them, and if he loves his food, then he will love eating his food from a treat dispenser like a KONG. Feeding your dog like this is a very easy way to put a daily challenge into his routine.

◉ Remember one bowl of food can be 50 tricks, 20 recalls, 10 KONGs or 30 minutes playing 'find it' in the garden, home, or wherever you take the time to hide the food. That bowl of food sounds pretty boring in comparison now, doesn't it? If you agree, then go into the kitchen now, throw away the bowl, and for dog's sake use the food!

CHAPTER 16
IN CONCLUSION

What kind of day has it been for your dog? When your dog goes to bed tonight, what will he be dreaming about? What wonderful things did he do today that made him feel like the happiest dog in town?

Your dog's perfect day

He drags himself out of bed when he hears you put the kettle on, and as happens every day, his wagging tail is the first thing to get a good workout. You both enjoy the five minutes you spend talking to him and stroking him. You notice some of the hair on his chest is a little dirty so you groom him. As usual he wants to play tuggy with your pyjamas when you take them off, but you easily distract him with a tennis ball, which he plays 'find it' with while you get dressed.

You only have time for a short walk, but you still manage to pack it full of challenge and fun, with lots of 'sits', 'downs', 'spins', and 'catch the treat' on your way to the nearest park. Then you take out his favourite Frisbee and you manage to wear him out in 10 minutes before you head back home.

He didn't even hear you leave for work because he was too busy munching on two of the three treat dispensers that you filled the previous evening. One of the KONGs contains that last small piece of steak from your tea that you didn't manage to finish. Or perhaps you left it on purpose, because you knew your dog would enjoy it in a KONG, and you knew that even though you were at work, you would still be able to contribute to his day. He finishes everything in the treat dispensers and sleeps until the dog walker comes to take him out for an hour.

You are happy with the new dog walker, who never walks too many dogs together and always plays games that keep the dogs focused on the human and not each other; this helps you with your training too. Then your dog enjoys the third KONG you filled and sleeps happily until you get home.

When you return from work, you sprinkle a handful of kibble into your garden so your dog can use his nose while you have a shower, then you take him out for an hour. You take a handful of treats to practise some heelwork, which is coming on well, and spend the first 10 minutes playing 'find the slipper', which you stuffed in your pocket before you left. He watches while you hide it behind a tree, and then to make it more difficult, you clip him back on lead and walk him 10 metres further away. Your dog loves this game so much, and you enjoy watching him nose the air and gradually move closer to the correct tree.

You notice a little rabbit jump out of a bush, but amazingly your dog doesn't seem to notice it at all. Unless he does notice but is too focused on the game, who knows? All you know is within five minutes of playing, the day's worries have melted away and you and your dog can enjoy a walk through the park safe inside your magic circle and not be disturbed by anyone or anything.

We are rapidly coming to the end of the book (your first read-through anyway), so what does the future look like now for you and your dog? A lot brighter, I would hope.

The average day I described above can be the perfect day for your dog, and I hope you think it's achievable for you. You can chop and change the activities and exercises to suit what your dog likes, but that's just details; the big idea is the same. Provide some challenge, be the fun, and use the things you know he likes, to play with, train, and entertain him. It's not that hard to do, and all you really need to commit is time and effort.

If you only complete half the activities I mentioned above, your dog will still be having all his daily doggy needs met, and then some. The chances are you and your dog will enjoy playing so much that you will play for longer than you intended anyway. The enjoyment in the game you play will grow like a snowball rolling down a hill, and then you will both look forward to the next session.

I have tried to strike a balance between giving you enough information to make an immediate difference to your life but not so much that you are overwhelmed. And that incidentally should be the same balance you try to achieve with your dog's training as you move forward. So give your dog enough of a challenge to make him think but also keep it fun enough so that he is engaged and his tail is always wagging. You will make mistakes along the way, but that's OK and is what is supposed to happen.

The main thing, though, is to stop reading and thinking and start doing.

When I first had the idea to write this book, I thought it would be a great way to help more dog owners who were struggling to connect with their dogs. My personal and online training clients had all achieved great success using the play methods I teach. Even the people who receive my dog training emails had started to enjoy more fun and focus with their dogs, and that was just a free 300-word daily story into their inbox. I tossed ideas around in my head for a few months, but every time I started, I got as far as writing a few pages before something else inevitably got in the way. The book, such as it was, got pushed to the back of my mind.

Then one day I just got serious about it. I invested in a book writing product that I thought would help me. And it helped a lot, not just with the planning and the writing and the advertising, but because now I had actually invested some money in the project. I had some skin in the game. Now I not only had a reason to write a book; I had a plan on how to do it. I was all set, right? Not really, I still had to actually start bloody writing.

I did that by dedicating a set time each day; early in the morning worked best for me. It wasn't easy – at first it was excruciating, and the first few weeks I wrote utter dross (I hope it's improved since then). But it gradually got easier, and I remembered how much I liked stories. I used to write loads when I was a kid, usually stories about the jungle or spacemen, and that was just for my mum and dad, but hey, it's all writing, so at least I would sell two copies, right?

I tell you this story to highlight the point that it's all about the doing. I wanted to write a book; you want to train your dog. I knew it would help people and help grow my business; you know that your life will be less stressful and more enjoyable if you do some training with your dog. I didn't know how to write a book; you didn't know how to train your dog. Then I had a plan and got inspiration from the book writing product. You have bought this book, and you know what you need to do to move forward (I also have some freebies and a special offer that will help you move forward more quickly, and the details for these are at the end of the book).

But, despite all the good intentions and the learning and the planning, at some point I still had to sit down and actually bloody write it. And unless you followed the exercises throughout the book, then that's where you are now too.

So my advice is to just do it. Start rewarding eye contact, and then move on from there. When it's done with fun, then dog training is infectious, and you want more of it. The most enjoyable part of my day is when I'm out spending time with my dogs and we can experience the great outdoors together, off lead, and I know I can call them back whenever I want. That's true freedom.

Even if that seems impossible at the moment, I hope you can see the potential to enjoy more freedom with your dog than you have right now.

Remember it's OK to want your dog to be better behaved, and you are the person best suited to the task of training him.

I mean, you spend most of your free time with your dog, you know all his good and bad points, and you love him more than anyone else on the planet. You are the perfect person to train your dog.

I hope this book will act as a springboard for you and your dog. Rather than trying to solve all the possible problems you may have with your dog, I have aimed to fix the main one, which to me is that most pet dog owners can't get their dogs to listen to them. But this should be the starting point for you to enjoy new activities with your dog. There are dog clubs all over the world that teach owners all kinds of activities. You could try anything from flyball to tracking, agility to heelwork to music and anything in between. Or if you are just happy to play with your own dog and keep him for yourself, then that's fine too.

Seven things to do today

Let's not waste any more time. If you are on board with everything (or most) of what I've been talking about for the last 200 or so pages, then let's make a big effort to improve things now. And here are seven things you can do today to begin transforming your relationship with your dog.

1) Identify all the places that stress you or your dog out. Or the place where he is most distracted and where you find it difficult to get his focus on you. Just DON'T GO THERE. Not for a while anyway, until he is more interested in you. But believe it or not, you actually get to decide where you take your dog each

day, and not taking him to the place where he embarrasses and frustrates you is a no-brainer.

2) Play. Play with your dog every day. You have instructions in this book for games aplenty. You can make up your own if you want, but please play with your dog. If there's one thing that always makes me smile, it's when I get an email from someone who has read my book and has begun to play with their dog more. They have immediately started to get more focus from their dog, and consequently they are enjoying walking their dog much more.

3) Find the Kryptonite. If you have no experience of training and don't know where to start, then finding the Kryptonite is going to give you an easy way into connecting and bonding with your dog. The Kryptonite could be anything, but try and make it something you can control (and carry). Take your time with this exercise, and have fun finding it too. Your dog may like the toy, but you make it special by the way you interact, so be playful.

4) Throw away the bowl. You can do this metaphorically or actually throw it away if you want. However, whichever you choose, your dog will thank you for it. Praise, affection, and toys are essential, but food is a powerful motivator for many dogs, so use it in as many ways as you can think of to play with, train, and entertain him. Treat your dog to some KONGs or other treat dispensers, and make him work for the food that he so craves. This will challenge your dog and get him using his nose and strong jaws. It lets him be a dog!

5) Get him using his nose. Your dog has superhuman abilities and can smell a worm farting in the garden next door. If you can control the nose, then you are halfway to controlling your dog. Start playing games where he finds food, toys, or people he loves. Make the 'find it' games easy at first. Try putting some food under a plastic plant pot, and watch your dog go from sleepy hound to sniffer dog. He's good at this, so challenge him to use his most powerful sense.

6) Give him a job. In simplest terms this means asking him to do something, and then pay him for it. Do this regularly and soon you will have your very own working pet dog that looks to you for all the good things in his life. A job can be anything from a 'sit' to finding your keys to carrying a ball home from the park. Once your dog has a series of jobs, tricks, and games to do throughout the day, he will go to bed tired and happy. And he will dream of the next day when he can do it all again.

7) Decide what you want from your pet dog. If you want him to be the playmate of every dog in town, well then, you know exactly how to achieve that, and you also have a pretty good idea what the consequences will be. But if you got a dog because you wanted a member of the family who will never answer back, complain about a lack of pocket money, go out and get drunk with his mates, and eventually meet someone, fall in love, and leave home, then you know how to achieve that too. Best friend, teacher, and superhero status are yours for the taking.

ACKNOWLEDGEMENTS

So it's done.

From start to finish it has taken me nine months in total. This is a tad longer than I wanted but does make it officially my baby. And as with all baby making, I couldn't have done it on my own, so here is a roundup of everyone who helped me on the journey.

The book

Jon McCulloch gets the blame for starting me off with the idea to write this book. I listened to 'that CD' for two months straight before I finally started writing, but I'm very glad I did because that was where the seed was sown.

Vicky Fraser helped me over the line with her rather excellent *Write and Publish Your Book in Just 90 Days* course. I bought the course on New Year's Eve and finished the actual writing just three months later, so it really does work. Thanks to both of you.

The writing turned out to be the easy part; it is the editing I found a complete bugger. The book wouldn't read nearly so well if it wasn't for the brilliant Jo Ciriani from the Spaghetti Agency, who edited, re-edited and polished it all to make it readable. Great work, Jo; we got there in the end!

Then there is the super-talented Julia King from Julia King Creative, who with the power of her pencils and PDFs turned me and Barry into superheroes. If people really do judge books by their covers, then they can't fail to be impressed by your wonderful work. And I love being a superhero, so thanks, Julia.

I must also mention Rebecca Ashworth from Sit, Stay, Capture Dog Photography for the back-cover image and my main man Alex Wardle from Artifact Media for all his help with PLTV and the Superhero Dog Owners Show Podcast and for the amazing filming and editing he does for the training videos inside the Superhero Dog Owners Inner Circle.

The dog trainers

I wouldn't be doing what I do with dogs if it wasn't for my good friend and mentor David Davies. I remember the first time I saw Dave demonstrating and playing with Hamish on John Rogerson's course and thinking to myself 'yes, that's the type of trainer I want to be'. I still do.

Thanks to John Rogerson, Dawn Cox, and Robert Alleyne too, for all you have taught me.

The business

The most important lesson I learned in the last year is to surround yourself with people who are smarter than you. You get the benefit of all of their experiences because they have done it all before, and this gets you to your goals much quicker than you would have done on your own. Yes, you have to pay for the help, but you should think of any coaching you pay for as an investment in yourself rather than a cost.

So, invest in yourself. Humans need to grow and progress, and you are worth it, so do it!

I've already mentioned Jon and Vicky, but there are some other key people who have had an immense impact on my business and personal life in the last 18 months. Here are a few more special people who have helped and continue to help me on my journey: Veronica Pullen, Dan Meredith, Ben Settle, and Mark 'Lord' Whitehand, you know what you did, so thanks very much.

The dogs

The best part of my working day is still when Alex and I are wandering along the Blast beach playing with the dogs, so I would like to give my heartfelt thanks to all my clients who have supported me over the last five years and for continuing to trust us with your precious dogs. You often say that we feel more like family than service providers, which fills me with pride.

Thanks especially to Amy and Craig Henderson and Lucy and Michael Garside for allowing me to use pictures of the handsome Stuey the Pug and pretty Aster the German Short-haired Pointer in the book.

The family

I've been extremely lucky throughout my whole life to have been surrounded by a very loving and funny family, who are always there for me, none more so than my Mam and Dad, thank you both.

Alex, my eldest, joined the business in 2015 and over the last year has stepped up and led the adventures, which has allowed me the time to complete the book. He is a brilliant lad and we laugh every day. Then there's our little 'dancing boy', Toby, who makes me smile every day, and my amazing wife, Beth, who has been there for me every step of the way. Team Hodge is going strong after 20 years, and I couldn't be happier.

And finally to Barry and Sid, who are still my favourite dogs to walk in the whole wide world.

A bit about me (and you)

Dog training is actually my third career. I left school with a handful of GCSEs and joined the theatre. It's true. Hi diddle dee dee, an actor's life for me. I sang and danced my way through my late teens before I settled down in my early twenties into my first 'proper job': a sales rep with a FTSE 100 company. I finished the last performance of *Sleeping Beauty* at the Tyne Theatre in Newcastle on a Sunday and started my sales training with Imperial Tobacco on the Monday. So I really did go from club singer to briefcase mong in the space of 24 hours. I learned a lot with that job, and then 10 years later I started my dog adventure business.

240

I couldn't be happier with how this latest venture has turned out. An idea became a plan and then a van full of dogs. Now I have a book, podcast, and my Superhero Dog Owners Inner Circle that helps dog owners all over the world to have more fun and really enjoy their dogs. What's next? Who knows? I'm just gonna work and play hard and see where it takes me.

So what's next for you? Well, that's up to you, isn't it?

To quote Ferris Bueller:

'Life moves pretty fast. If you don't stop and look around once in a while, you could miss it.'

True dat.

Don't forget to stop now and again. The greatest gift you can give your dog, your family, your friends, and yourself is time, so stop and play with your dog. Try and make time to play with your dog every single day. Place the same importance on playing with your dog as you do on eating, sleeping, and paying the mortgage. Then see how you can play more in other parts of your life. Just like you did with the dog audit, you can quickly identify things or people that cause you the most stress, and remove them from your life.

So stop and look around. Decide what you really want from life, and take a small step every day that will move you closer to your goal.

Start today...

BARRY'S BAKING BONUS

You know by now that 'Yorkies' are Barry's numero-uno Kryptonite, and they are also the favourite thing on my Sunday dinner plate too.

If you have never had a Yorkshire pudding before, then here's your chance to give them a go. They are traditionally served with a roast dinner but also go well with any casserole-type dish that has gravy. Oh, and if you have tried and failed with them before, then this recipe will get you back on track and make you the darling of the dinner table.

You can buy part-baked frozen Yorkshire puddings, but Barry thinks they are the devil's work, and I agree. In my humble, honest, and correct opinion, you are much better off spending five minutes knocking up your own, using this foolproof recipe. Remember if it's easy enough for Dom to do, then it's easy enough for you too.

Ingredients

300 grams plain flour
150 mls milk
150 mls water
3 eggs (medium/large)
Pinch of salt
Vegetable oil

Instructions

- ◉ Put the salt in a large mixing bowl then add the flour, two whole eggs, and one egg yolk.

- ◉ Mix the water and milk in a jug and slowly pour into the bowl, whisking the mixture at the same time.

- ◉ I like to add a little of the milk and water and then whisk for 10 seconds then add a little more and repeat until almost all of the liquid is mixed in with the eggs and flour. You are looking for a consistency close to single cream.

- ◉ Then pour the mixture into the jug and leave to stand for at least 30 minutes. You should have around 500 mls of the mixture, which is enough to make around 18 puds. We use two baking trays – one with enough for 12 and another for six.

The cooking

- ◉ Pre-heat the oven for 10 mins to around 220°C or gas mark 7 then pour a tablespoon or two of the vegetable oil into each tray and put the tray into the oven to preheat for at least 10 mins.

◎ Using your oven gloves, carefully take out the hot baking trays and half-fill each bowl with the Yorkshire pudding batter. The oil should be spitting hot, and the batter should sizzle when you pour it in.

◎ Then put back in the oven and wait around 20 minutes.

◎ Check after 20 minutes, but don't be tempted to look before then, as you will let the heat escape, and we want it nice and hot in the oven to give the puddings the best chance to rise.

◎ I like mine to be quite dark in colour, so sometimes anything up to another five minutes may be needed.

Then remove from the oven, allow them to cool, and let everyone marvel at your magnificent, fluffy Yorkies.

HOW TO CONTACT THE AUTHOR

Upon invitation I am available for speaking engagements and to deliver seminars. I always enjoy visiting dog training clubs, where I can lead a variety of training sessions and workshops and you can learn in more detail how to be your dog's superhero and have more fun with your dog.

For more advice on how you can have more fun with your dog, you should check out my **Superhero Dog Owners Show on iTunes**. This is a weekly video podcast where you can learn how to have more fun with your pet dog. You can subscribe on iTunes by searching for the Superhero Dog Owners Show.

Due to my busy schedule, I am only available to take on a small number of private training clients at any one time. If you would like some more intensive training to help you with some problems you are having with your dog and wish to become a private training client, you should email **hello@packleaderdogadventures.co.uk**

You will be added to my priority waiting list. This is the only way you can book an appointment to work with me privately.

For all media enquiries including print, TV, and radio, please email **hello@packleaderdogadventures.co.uk**

If you are a dog trainer who has enjoyed *How To Be Your Dog's Superhero* and you wish to obtain copies in bulk at a substantial discount to give as gifts to your own training clients, then please email me at

hello@packleaderdogadventures.co.uk

A SPECIAL FREE GIFT FOR YOU

How To Be Your Dog's Superhero contains everything you need to help you solve the most crucial problem most dog owners have and that is how to get your dog to focus and listen to you. But I understand that I'm not able to go into enough detail on every aspect of how to do this, so to help kick- start your dog training and make it even easier for you to take action, I am giving you free access to one of my most powerful dog training videos.

This is my gift to you for having the courage and responsibility to change your dog's behaviour.

How To Find Your Dog's Kryptonite

According to the clients inside my inner circle, this is one of the most powerful and useful training videos I have done. If you struggle to get your dog's attention, then this is the training you have been looking for. *How To Find Your Dog's Kryptonite* will give you a more detailed overview of exactly how you can identify and use that elusive thing your dog likes, to play with and train him.

To access this fun and free training go to:
www.mydogssuperhero.com/bonus and I will see you on
the inside…

OTHER BOOKS BY THE AUTHOR

Street-Smart Dog Training Series (1–3)

Worry Free Walks – How to transform your difficult, dangerous and devilish dog into a problem-free pooch you are proud to take to the park.

The Perfect Puppy Recipe – The first time puppy owners step by step guide for a no-stress, no-mess, problem-free puppy.

The Hungry Games – Discover how you can bin the bowl and use the food to play, train and entertain your perfect pet dog.

Pet Business Books

Walk Yourself Wealthy: The quick, easy and no-BS guide to transform your passion for pooches into an insanely profitable and fun dog-walking empire.

Printed by Amazon Italia Logistica S.r.l.
Torrazza Piemonte (TO), Italy

11410560R00153